Where Your Tax Dollar Goes...

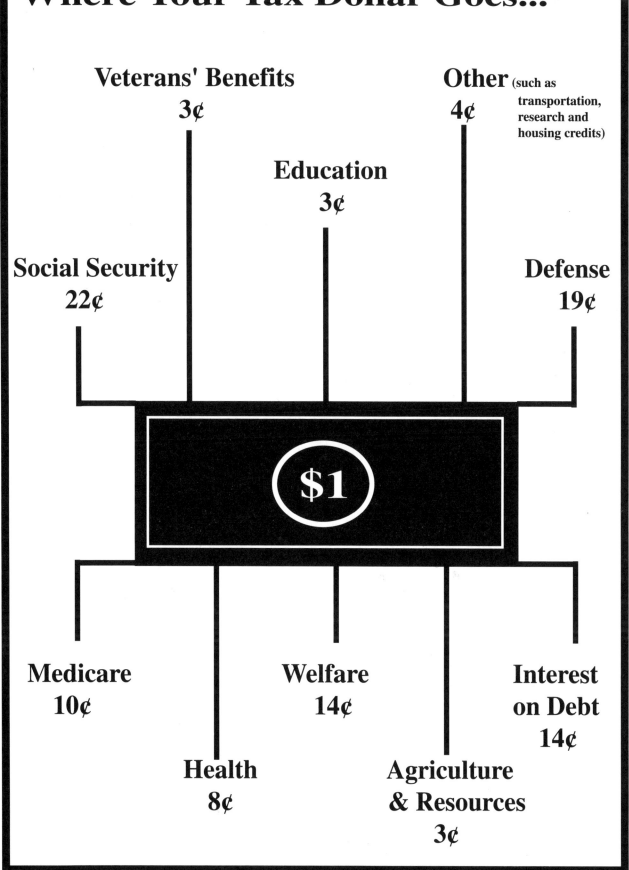

Every effort has been made by the author to provide completely accurate and timely data and any changes in the information herein occurred after the information in this publication was gathered and printed.

This book was originally published in 1994 by the author. It is reprinted with corrections by arrangement with the author.

First HarperBusiness edition published 1995.

ISBN 0-88730-775-2

95 96 97 98 99 10 9 8 7 6 5 4 3 2 1

The First Annual Report of the United States of America

CONTENTS

Taking Responsibility

A Letter to the American People

"Since World War II we have gone from the world's largest creditor nation to the world's largest debtor nation."

"....never in the history of the world has a debtor nation been able to maintain its power."

All of us have moments that change our lives. That moment came for me as I was sitting in a classroom finishing my second year at Harvard. An economics concentrator, I was attending a macroeconomics class taught by Professor Benjamin Friedman.

For many, economics can be a very dry subject and one which does not touch our emotions; however, something that my professor said that day pounded my emotions. In closing he said, "America is undergoing one of the most critical periods in its history. Since World War II we have gone from the world's largest creditor nation to the world's largest debtor nation.

"We have run a debt which currently equals 80% of our Gross Domestic Product. We are faced with sky-rocketing deficits that do not appear to be coming down. In short, if we continue along the path that we are now there is the great possibility of bankruptcy."

He went on, "It is true that America is the only hegemonic power in the world now. We have defeated the USSR in the cold war. We are the only nation capable of defending democracy, capable of launching any substantial war, the only nation with a strong military, a strong infrastructure. But," he added words of warning, "never in the history of the world has a debtor nation been able to maintain its power." These are the words that led me to produce this report.

As a child, as a teenager and as a college student, I was always taught to believe that America was the greatest nation to live in, that we were the nation with the most opportunity and the highest economic prosperity for all and that in the global context America held the world's hope for freedom. As an adult, I see the status that America once gripped rapidly diminishing. One has only to look at the example of Rome or the Imperial Empire of Great Britain or the once Ottoman Empire of the East to realize that all great nations and all great empires come to an end if they cannot diagnose and cure themselves from within.

I feel a great urgency to try to reverse that seemingly inevitable end. I ask you to join me in taking responsibility to change the course of America.

The symptoms of this ailing society are stark. We have unbelievable amounts of debt. We have an ever growing bureaucracy which takes decisions, money and power out of the hands of citizens. But, worst of all, we, the American people, feel helpless.

In the following pages, I present what I have found in my research to be our most troubling concerns so that we may begin to understand what has gone wrong and how we may be able to make things better.

The book is separated into five main sections. Financial Highlights, Economic State of the Nation and the Financial Review all detail our economic status. The Social State of the Nation and the International State of the Nation speak of important trends which are affecting the way we live our every day life.

In my presentation, I have tried to be nonpartisan because I believe that party politics often clouds and distorts the real issues at stake. I believe that the state of our nation is not merely the Democrats' or the Republicans' fault, but everyone's responsibility. If we will ever succeed as a nation, we must stop blaming one another and start coming up with solutions.

I have found that the most pressing issues facing America are:

(1) We have a huge debt which is draining funds out of the private sector and which is compromising our growth and our position as a world power.

(2) There is a growing inequality in America which is pushing more and more people to the fringes of society. Young families, single mothers, and children of every age are increasingly having to deal with the ravages

"The symptoms of this ailing society are stark."

"...worst of all, we, the American people, feel helpless."

4

of poverty.

(3)We save very little compared to other industrialized nations. Because of this habit there is little money to invest in our future.

(4)We invest very little in education. We have a good college system, but our public grade schools and high schools produce adults that increasingly cannot read and do not have the skills to compete in a now global marketplace.

(5)Crime and drug use are on the rise not just in our cities, but throughout our nation. Citizens are beginning to try to defend themselves, starting volunteer patrol organizations and increasing their purchase of weapons.

(6)The U.S. faces complex problems internationally as nations break apart and reunite, literally changing the face of the globe overnight. The U.S. must equip itself to deal with new military threats and difficult economic challenges (such as the Mexican monetary problem).

(7) The U.S. is burdened with huge social programs which are financially crippling our nation such as Social Security, Health Care,Medicare and Medicaid. No one wants to deal with these issues because they are politically explosive.

Any one of these problems could threaten the very existence of the United States of America. Together they are fatal. Fatal, that is, if we let them fester. As the great statesman, Edmund Burke, said, "All that is necessary for evil to triumph is for good men to do nothing."

I know from the letters that I have received after publishing this report that the American people do care deeply about our nation. It is now our job to muster that desire and send it to Washington.

This is why I offer you *The First Annual Report of the United States of America.*

"Any one of these problems could threaten the very existence of the United States of America. Together they are fatal. Fatal, that is, if we do nothing."

"You are a shareholder in America"

You are a shareholder in America because it is your taxes that pay for all federal programs -- from highways to military weapons. In any corporation stockholders receive an annual report to show them what has happened to their investment. We have never seen such a report directed to us as stockholders of this nation.

The people who led this nation in its infancy and who conceptualized what America could be knew that an informed population is the keystone of a democracy. Today we are bombarded with more media than our forefathers could have ever imagined, but the quality of information coming at us is generally superficial, biased to the right or left or sheer entertainment.

Through this report I hope to help you enter or re-enter the political process. For too long we have allowed our nation to run on bureaucratic pilot. We have not been conscientious voters and, indeed, many of us have not voted at all. The only way to have a true democracy, as Thomas Jefferson said, is to be active in it and be educated. We must learn about our nation through individual initiative. This annual report seeks to inform you generally about our economic, social and international position so that you will hold our leaders accountable for the future they are creating for us.

As 1995 grows to its maturity and yields to 1996, the Congress and the President will be creating our future in their decisions on the budget and on new legislation. I urge you to use these facts and figures to question your government, interact with it and make America safe, healthy and vibrant again.

MEREDITH E. BAGBY

"The people who led this nation in its infancy ...knew that an informed population is the keystone of a democracy. "

"I urge you to use these facts and figures to question your government, interact with it and make America safe, healthy and vibrant again."

Family Type

The traditional family, a working father with a mother who stays home, is on the decline. Most families are now dual career. The number of single-mother families has also risen since the 1950s.

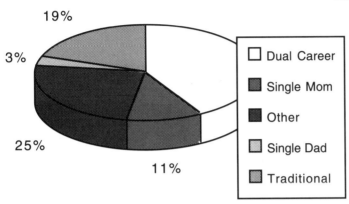

42%

19%

3%

25%

11%

- ☐ Dual Career
- ■ Single Mom
- ■ Other
- ▨ Single Dad
- ▨ Traditional

The United States of America is a nation of 260 million in a world of 5.7 billion people. We are a diverse nation of people coming from every nation and every race that exists. Though from different backgrounds, we are unified by a common work ethic, a belief in human freedom and a mutual desire to make life better for all of us. We consist of 50 states and the District of Columbia, American Samoa, Baker Island and Jarvis Island, Guam, Howland Island, Johnston Island and Sand Island, Kingman Reef, Midway Island, Northern Mariana Islands, Palmyra Island, Puerto Rico, Trust Territory of the Pacific Islands, Virgin Islands of the U. S. and Wake Island.

What Mom Is Doing

This graph of a typical day shows how a mother spends her time. Since Mom went to work, she has less time to cook, to do chores and to spend with her husband and children than her mother did. She does, however, spend more time at work and on personal matters than did her mother's generation .

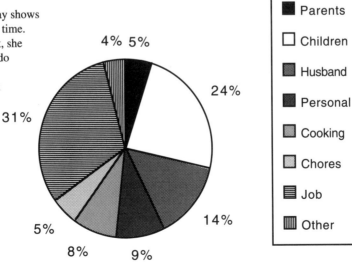

4% 5%

24%

31%

5%

8%

9%

14%

- ■ Parents
- ☐ Children
- ▨ Husband
- ■ Personal
- ▨ Cooking
- ▨ Chores
- ▤ Job
- ▥ Other

Statistics About America...

Percent of the Work Force

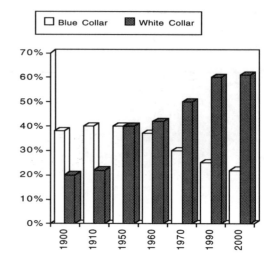

The Labor Force

1960
Total= 66 million

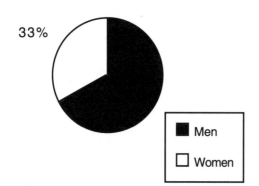

33%

■ Men
☐ Women

As time moves on, the American work force depends more and more on white collar jobs. The well-paying blue collar jobs which accounted for America's increased living standards for so long have been and continue to be on the downfall while white collar jobs are on the rise.

The biggest change in the makeup of the labor force in the past 30 years is the entrance of women. Today women make up almost half of the labor force.

1990
Total = 117 million

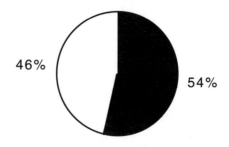

46%   54%

Just over half of eligible voters participated in the last presidential election. While this is a low turnout, the percentage is up from the last three presidential elections and higher than the turnouts for Congressional or state elections.

Voters and Nonvoters for President in 1992

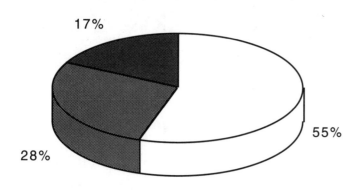

17%

28%

55%

☐ Voted for   Registered but   ■ Didn't register
  president   didn't vote

8

Where America Lives

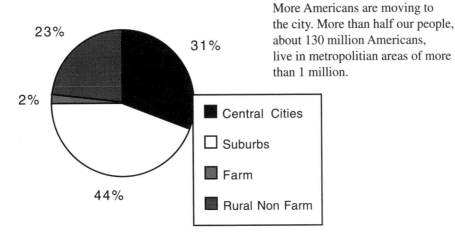

23%

31%

2%

44%

- ■ Central Cities
- □ Suburbs
- ▨ Farm
- ■ Rural Non Farm

More Americans are moving to the city. More than half our people, about 130 million Americans, live in metropolitian areas of more than 1 million.

Median Family Income

$35,939

Average Earnings per Hour

Education is becomimg a more important determinant of future salaries. As demand rises for educated and skilled workers, the price paid to those with high education rises and the price paid to lesser educated workers falls.

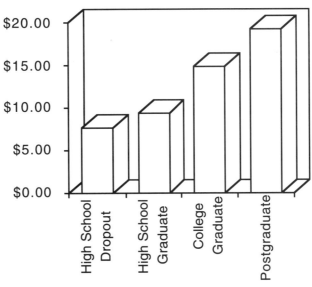

$20.00

$15.00

$10.00

$5.00

$0.00

High School Dropout

High School Graduate

College Graduate

Postgraduate

Who We Are

The United States Budget

Net Income: The money that the government collects.

Most of this money comes from taxes of which there are many kinds.

(millions of dollars)

	(actual) 1993	(estimates) 1994	1995
Individual Income Taxes	$509,680	$549,901	$595,048
Corporation Income Taxes	$117,520	$130,719	$140,437
Excise Taxes	$48,057	$54,550	$71,888
Social Insurance Taxes	$428,300	$461,923	$490,393
Custom Duties	$18,802	$19,198	$20,856
Estate and Gift Taxes	$12,577	$12,749	$13,885
NET INCOME	**$1,153,535**	**$1,249,071**	**$1,353,815**

Individual Income Tax

A tax levied on your salary and any other profit you make, for instance, in the stock market or from your savings account.

Corporate Income Tax.

A tax levied on corporate profits. What McDonald's has to pay.

Excise Taxes

A tax levied on certain commodities like tobacco or alcohol. Excise taxes tend to be popular politically. For instance, many suggest that we tax cigarettes so that we encourage people to smoke less. We also put excise taxes on oil so that people will consume less gas.

Social Insurance Tax

A tax taken out of wages before the salary ever reaches the individual. The money then put in a fund goes to pay for the Social Security benefits of the elderly, retired and disabled. The tax exists to ensure that people will have something to live on once they become too old to work. It is a kind of forced savings.

Estate and Gift Taxes

Estate taxes are put on personal property at the time of death. Gift taxes are levied on large gifts given from one person to another.

Customs Duties

Taxes put on food and goods coming into the U.S. For instance, the tax on Japanese cars.

Where Taxes Come From

Most taxes come from individual income taxes followed by Social Security tax and corporate income tax.

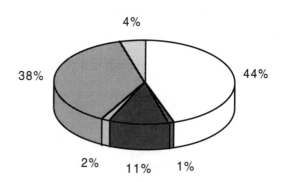

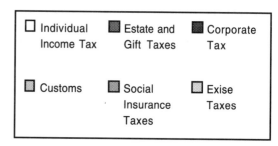

10

Net Expenses:

Anything that the government spends. It includes everything from the cost of building roads to the president's salary to grants to research and development. The government spends our money in essentially two ways: transfer payments and service payments.

(millions of dollars)

	(actual) 1993	(estimates) 1994	1995
Service Payments			
International Affairs	$16,826	$18,968	$17,798
Judiciary	$14,955	$16,479	$17,331
Science/Technology	$17,030	$17,279	$16,941
Transportation	$35,004	$37,582	$38,368
Natural Resources	$20,239	$22,285	$21,817
Defense	$291,086	$279,824	$270,725
Education	$50,012	$50,793	$53,524
Energy	$4,319	$4,988	$4,564
Health	$99,415	$112,252	$123,077
Community Development	$9,051	$9,282	$9,154
Transfer Payments			
Social Security	$304,585	$320,460	$337,168
Housing Credit	-$22,725	-$504	-$5,482
Medicare	$130,552	$143,651	$156,228
Income Security	$207,257	$214,626	$221,440
Veterans' Benefits	$35,720	$38,129	$39,247
Interest on the Public Debt	$198,811	$203,448	$212,835
Net Expenses	**$1,408,205**	**$1,483,829**	**$1,518,945**
DEFICIT	**$254,670**	**$234,758**	**$165,130**

Transfer Payments

Transfer payments occur when the government transfers money from one group in society to another, for example when the government taxes the general public in order to give money to the poor in the form of welfare or when the government gives money to the elderly in the form of Social Security.

Some other transfer payments are the Commerce and Housing Credit which gives money to people who cannot provide housing for themselves. Another example is Medicare which provides health care for the elderly.

Service Payments

Service payments occur when the government buys a particular service for the U.S. Examples include building roads, providing for our national defense or investing in science by financing a space shuttle.

Net Interest

Net interest is the amount we pay each year on our debt. In simple terms, it is this amount that the goverment has to pay for taking out loans.

Goverment pays interest by meeting its obligations on U.S. bonds or bills sold to investors. Each year that amount gets larger because each year the U.S. accumulates more debt.

Deficit

This is income minus expenses or the amount the federal government takes in from taxes subracting the amount that the federal goverment spends. For the last 25 years this number has been negative. The new budget bill passed in 1993 seeks to reduce the deficit by 1998 by cutting spending and increasing taxes.

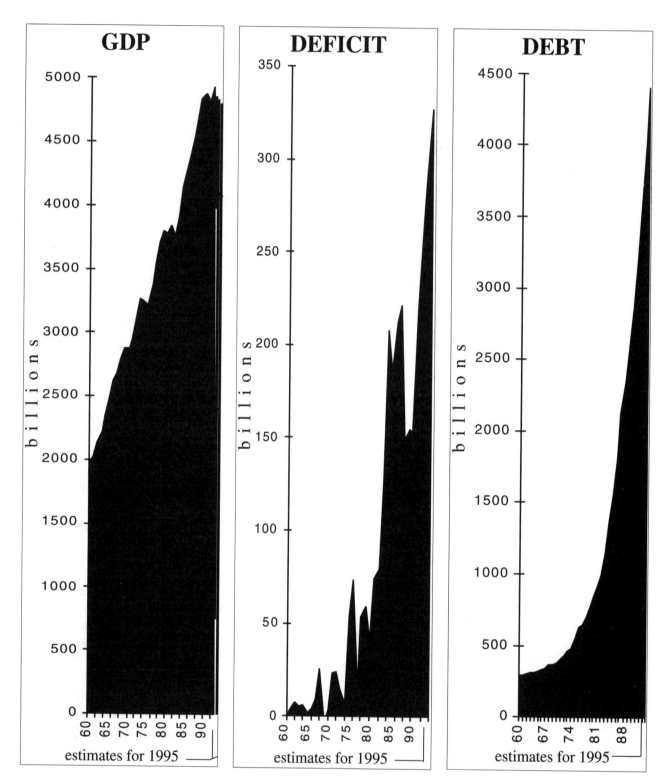

GDP

5000
4500
4000
3500
3000
2500

b i l l i o n s

2000
1500
1000
500
0

60 65 70 75 80 85 90

estimates for 1995

DEFICIT

350
300
250
200

b i l l i o n s

150
100
50
0

60 65 70 75 80 85 90

estimates for 1995

DEBT

4500
4000
3500
3000
2500

b i l l i o n s

2000
1500
1000
500
0

60 67 74 81 88

estimates for 1995

GROSS DOMESTIC PRODUCT
The graph shows the GDP or gross domestic product. GDP has risen fairly
consistently from 1960 to 1995. However, in the past few years --1990 - 1995
-- that growth has slowed and has even
been negative from 1990 - 1991 when
America was in a recession.

FEDERAL GOVERMENT DEFICIT
The U.S. deficit has increased most
noticeably from 1980 onward. On the
vertical axis you will see that in 1993 our
deficit was about $260 billion dollars.

FEDERAL GOVERMENT DEBT
The debt in this chart shows that the
federal government owes almost as
much money as our entire nation pro-
duces each year. For the U.S. this enor-
mous debt is a modern problem and the
foremost and primary concern for our
economic stability.

12

An Overview of Our Problems...

America seems to be facing one of its most difficult economic periods in its history. Although America still has a better quality of life than nearly any nation on earth, we have deep fiscal problems which may soon undermine our economic well-being and our ability to maintain world leadership for democracy.

While U.S. workers and firms remain the world's most productive, **our productivity growth has been sluggish for almost two decades**. As a direct result, wages and family incomes have advanced extremely slowly — possibly making Generation X, the people presently in their twenties and teens, the first generation in America to have a lower standard of life than their parents.

In addition, it seems that the rich are getting richer and the poor are becoming poorer. We have a shrinking middle class as **families get pulled to the fringes of either poverty or wealth**. The National Council of Economic Advisors reports that over the last decade many middle-class and low-income families have actually experienced declines in their real incomes.

Furthermore, the federal budget deficit has been growing and the **national debt has outpaced our growth** rate for nearly a decade. Our extensive foriegn borrowing to finance this debt has transformed the U.S. from the largest creditor nation in the world to the biggest debtor.

Financial Highlights

IMPORTANT TERMS DEFINED

GDP - stands for gross domestic product and it is the sum of all of the production of goods and services in America for a particular year. GDP is important because it is a measure of how productive we are as a nation. Furthermore, by comparing GDP from year to year we can examine the rates at which we are improving our production.

Deficit - tells us how much the U.S. goverment spends beyond what it makes in taxes. The U.S. has been consistently running a deficit since 1960.

Debt - is money the government borrows, usually to finance the accumulation of the deficit. Debt is the amount that the government owes either to its people or to foreign countries and institutions that invest in U.S. treasuries and other securities. Presently the U.S. is the world's largest debtor. Each year the U.S. has to pay interest on this debt just as you or I do when we borrow from a bank. The interest payment on the national debt is larger than the entire gross national product of Mexico.

The Balance Sheet of the President's Budget

Major Cuts

Discretionary Programs (such as defense, education, transportation and environment):	$101 billion
Mandatory Programs (such as Social Security, Medicare, etc.)	$29 billion
Tax Compliance	$9 billion
Debt Service	$5 billion
TOTAL NEW CUTS	**$144 billion**

Major New Spending

Defense	$25.0 billion
Crime Control	$3.4 billion
Drug Abuse Control	$1.3 billion
Immigration Concerns	$1.0 billion
Environmental Cleanup	$1.0 billion
National Service	$.29 billion
Other	$31.0 billion
TOTAL SPENDING	**$63 billion**

REDUCTION IN DEFICIT	**$81 billion (in 1996)**

How the Middle-Class Tax Cut Might Affect You...

• A $500 per child tax credit for middle-income families with children under 13.

• An increased eligibility for Individual Retirement Accounts (IRAs) and an allowance for families to make penalty-free withdrawals for a range of educational, housing or medical needs.

• A tax deduction for the costs of college, university or vocational education.

• A G.I. Bill for America's workers by consolidating 70 job training programs and using the money to offer "skill grants" through which dislocated and low-income workers can make their own choices about the training they need.

Party Responses to the President's Budget

On the whole, Democrats have applauded Clinton's budget proposal. The Republicans want a more drastic change in the way the government spends its money.

The Republicans are in favor of (1) more spending cuts, particularly social programs, (2) more tax breaks and (3) a balanced budget amendment (i.e., an amendment to the constitution which would force the Congress to spend no more money than it takes in each year in taxes.)

The Democrats argue that a balanced budget amendment would be dangerous because it would limit the government's ability to react to certain crises which may demand fiscal spending such as a banking crisis.

The Budget for Proposal 1996

President Clinton sent Congress his fiscal 1996 budget on February 6, 1995. This budget has four important measures: (1) tax reduction for middle-income Americans, (2) deficit reduction through terminating 131 government programs and cutting 86 other programs, (3) an increase in some spending for education, research in science and technology and a defense restructuring called the Defense Funding Initiative and (4) an increase in minimum wage from $4.25 to $5.15.

Of the $144 billion in cuts, $81 billion will go toward deficit reduction. This reduction comes on top of the President's 1993 deficit reduction plan (OBRA93: see pp.15-16). The other $63 billion will go to new spending and tax cuts for the middle class.

The Republican Congress has the ability to reform and change the President's Budget Plan. So far, the Congress has voted to boost defense spending $3.2 billion in order to increase "combat readiness and peacekeeping" and to cut domestic programs like youth job training.

In addition, the House Appropriations Subcommitee on Labor, Health and Human Services has proposed cuts in education, job training, fuel assistance, Head Start, and a nutrition program for pregnant women, infants and children. These cuts are meant to pay for deficit reduction and possible tax cuts.

Spending on Selected Government Programs
As proposed by the Clinton Budget

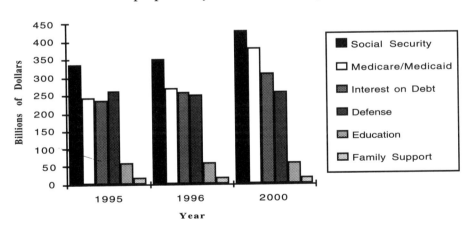

Despite budget reform, expenditures on Social Security, Medicare, Medicaid and the interest on the debt will continue to increase into the next century. Funds going to defense, education and family support remain flat. Under a Republican budget plan, funds to education, welfare, family support and environmental cleanup would likely fall. Defense spending would increase more than the President has proposed and Social Security spending will likely continue to rise.

Financial Highlights

Deficit in Billions of Dollars

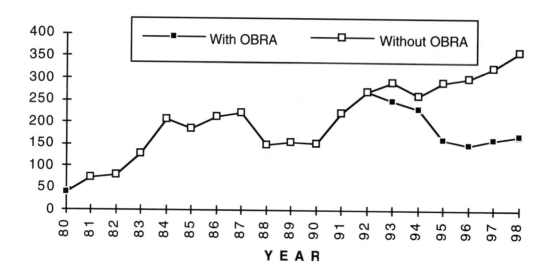

The deficit will decrease with the implemenation of the president's new budget bill but will not disappear. Even with Omnibus Budget Reconciliation Act of 1993 (OBRA 93), the deficit may resume its upward trend after 1997.

Debt as a Percentage of GDP

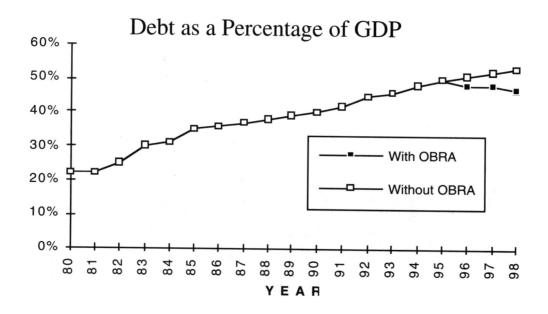

As the graph shows, OBRA 93 will put only a small dent in our debt problem. Regardless of the spending cuts and tax hikes, our debt will still remain well above 40% of our gross domestic product and we will likely still remain the world's biggest debtor nation.

Omnibus Budget Reconciliation Act of 1993 (OBRA 93)

After his first few weeks in office, President William Clinton proposed a budget plan to a joint session of Congress. OBRA 93, as it is called, was aimed at reducing the U.S. deficit. According to the plan, the deficit will be reduced by $146 billion by 1998. This reduction consists of $87 billion in net spending cuts and $59 billion in added revenue from taxes.

The government "reduced" spending by putting caps on every aspect of the budget: The government will not increase

---

The OBRA 93 Balance Sheet
(in billions)

$87 reduced spending
+ $59 new taxes

$146 reduced in deficit

---

spending on any portion of the budget. The largest cuts were felt in Medicare (about $18 billion by 1998). Furthermore, the

Congress increased taxes on the richest 6.5% of the population.

While OBRA 93 will certainly help reduce the deficit, as we can see by the graph opposite, it will not eliminate the deficit but merely hold it at bay. Even with the reforms, the deficit will still be over 150 billion dollars a year. As we can also see by the graph charting debt, the reforms do nothing to decrease debt. Debt continues to increase throughout the rest of the decade.

All of these projections are offered by the administration itself and are thus relatively optimistic. The situation might even be worse. Many argue that the president will not be able to realize so much new tax revenue as he expects if the rich are able to to hide their money and, thus, avoid paying higher taxes. All in all, OBRA 93 makes only a small dent in a trillion-dollar problem.

How the New Taxes Affect You...

• *High brackets for top earners* — a new tax bracket of 36 % applies to taxable income exceeding the following amounts and is retroactive to January 1993.

Single	$115,000
Head of household	$127,500
Couple filing jointly	$140,000
Married, filing separately	$70,000

• *10 % surtax* — applies to certain high-income taxpayers. It is computed by applying a 39.6% rate to taxable income in excess of $250,000 for individuals or $125,000 for married couples filing separately.

• *Limits* — are put on itemized tax deductions and there is a phase-out of personal exemptions for high earners .

• *No Medicare tax limit* — beginning January 1994, you pay a 1.45% on Medicare tax on your first $135,000 of salary and on all earned income. Self-employed people will pay 2.9% to compensate for the lack of an employer's contribution.

• *Taxes on Social Security income* — hit harder. Once a retired couple's income tops $44,000 ($34,000 for individuals), up to 85% of their Social Security benefits will be taxed.

For more information see Financial Review .

Financial Highlights

Taking America's Pulse...

VITAL SIGNS

	1992	1993	1994	1995	1996	1997	1998
	Percent change, fourth quarter to fourth quarter						
Real Gross Domestic Product	2.6	2.9	3.1	3.0	4.0	3.4	3.2
Consumer Price Index	2.9	2.8	2.9	3.0	3.0	3.0	3.0
	Calendar year average						
Unemployment Rate	7.4	6.9	6.2	5.7	5.4	5.3	5.3
Interest Rate 91-day Treasury Bills	3.4	3.5	4.2	4.4	4.4	4.4	4.4
Interest rate 10-year Treasury Notes	7.0	6.4	6.1	6.0	6.0	6.0	6.0

The Bad News

The recovery from the recession of 1990 and 1991 has been the slowest and most difficult recovery for America in its post-war history. Growth remained slow, unemployment remained high and consumer demand low throughout 1992 and most of 1993. This slow recovery can be attributed to several different factors.

First, unemployment remained high. America drastically cut back on defense spending thus sending thousands into long-term unemployment. American corporations began downsizing and restructuring. With rapid technology and corporate restructuring on the rise, many found that their jobs no longer existed. This sent many in search of new training and different kinds of jobs.

Furthermore, overly tight regulations on banks because of a backlash from the savings and loan crisis has made it hard to borrow money. In addition, the U.S. goverment, in order to finance its large debt, is sucking up a lot of available American and international investment funds that would otherwise go to private business.

America, in comparison to the fastest growing industrialized economies, has invested little over the past two decades in infrastructure, research, technology and education. As economists tell us, these are the main components of economic growth.

Finally, the U.S. trade balance has been becoming increasingly negative since 1991 despite the fact that the U.S. dollar has droped in value in comparison to foreign currencies (seemingly making it cheaper for foreigners to buy U.S. products and thus boosting exports).

In 1994 the trade balance was about -$100 billion as compared to -$14 billion in 1991. This means that we are importing $100 billion more in foreign goods than we are selling of U.S. exports.

18

The Good News

Since 1993 the growth rate has picked up. In the third quarter of 1994, current-dollar gross domestic product rose 6.2 percent and real GDP rose 4.0 percent. (The change in real GDP means the difference between last year and this year acounting for inflation.)

Futhermore, over the past year unemployment has been on its way down. The administration projects that by 1997 unemployment will drop to 5.3%. According to many economists, this rate is close to the full-employment level (i.e.,those who seek work will be able to find work in a few months).

More good news is that the U.S. is experiencing low inflation rates. Low inflation engenders confidence about the economy and preserves the value of our assets. While inflation rose slightly in 1994, rates are still historically low.

Althougth interst rates increased in 1994 and 1995 they are still relatively low compared to the late 1980s and early 1990s. In addition, it is likely that interest rates will decrease slightly over the next year.

At lower interest rates, both businesses and families are able to borrow money more cheaply to begin new ventures --such as buying a home or building a warehouse. All of this is good for the stock market.

Finally, America has increased its productivity per worker over the past five years. Corporate restructuring along with macroeconomic forces such as international competition has produced a leaner more efficient workforce.

U.S. Trade

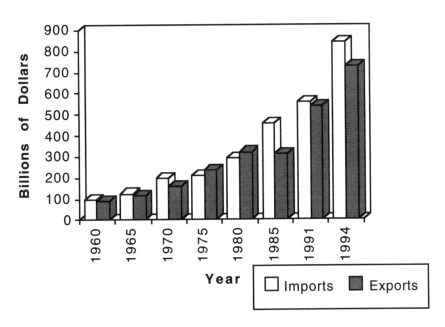

Throughout the 1980s exports fell short of imports-- we bought more foreign goods than we sold. This was in part because the strong dollar made imports relatively cheap for the U.S. and made U.S. imports relatively expensive abroad. It is also important to recognize that U.S. trade has increased substantially since 1960, now making up more than 30 percent of our entire economy.

Financial Highlights

HEALTH CARE

Americans are living longer, healthier lives than ever before. Since 1960 the average life expectancy has increased by more than 5 years. Furthermore, America leads the world in medical research and the quality of medical care. American physicians have access to the best medical technology in the world and more than one-half of the world's medical research is funded by sources in America.

At the same time, AIDS claimed the lives of more than 160,000 Americans last year. Tuberculosis, a disease that had almost disappeared in the United States, has re-emerged. Cancer, heart disease and strokes are the leading causes of death in the United States, together accounting for about two-thirds of all fatalities.

But the biggest problems in health care are (1) that health care costs are soaring much faster than the general inflation rate and (2) there are 35 million Americans who are not insured and even more who do not receive proper medical care.

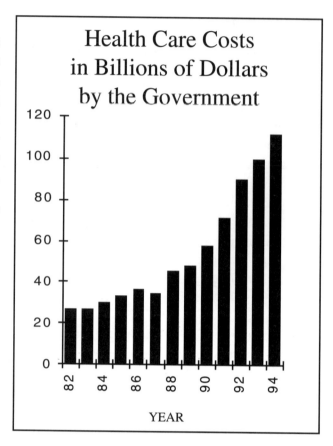

Soaring Costs

The share of the nation's income devoted to health care has been growing rapidly. The United States spends far more per capita on health care than does any other country on earth. One dollar out of every seven dollars spent goes toward health care. The increases reflect higher prices for medical services and the greater use of more sophisticated treatments and services.

The system of health insurance, third-party payment and the lack of incentives to use health services wisely are only a few of the factors that are driving up health care costs. As health care now consumes roughly 25% of the gross domestic product and yet still provides little or no care to many Americans, there is a need for reform.

Health Insurance

According to 1991 Census Bureau data, there are approximately 35 million Americans without health insurance. This means that one out of every seven or eight Americans is not covered by health insurance. The majority of the uninsured seems to be young adults and children of uninsured adults. The uninsured receive insufficient preventative care and often end up flooding emergency rooms.

Most Americans are insured through their employers. Employer-provided insurance benefits have increased dramatically since WW II. A recent survey found that more than 25% of American households included a family member who stayed in a job because of health coverage restrictions. Many employees now pay for increases in health care costs mainly through lower wages. Many of the uninsured workers employed by small firms earn wages which, if the wages were reduced by the cost of health insurance, would fall below minimum wage.

Reform

In campaign speeches, President Clinton promised the American people a complete health care reform package. This package would include universal coverage, employer mandates, price controls on health care and nondiscrimination rules for insurance companies. Many, even in the president's Democratic party, believe that the president's plan creates too much bureaucracy and puts too many restrictions on individual choice.

Since the president presented his plan to Congress, more than 70 new plans have been proposed ranging from a market-based approach to a completely government-run health insurance program.

Future Legislation

One can only guess what health care reform will look like in the future. However, it seems that the main aims of health reform are:

(1) to reduce the cost of medical care by increasing efficiency. Probably people will be encouraged to see primary care physicians rather than more expensive specialists. There will be an emphasis on preventative care to avoid expensive emergency room visits.

(2) to extend coverage to as many Americans as possible. This will likely be accomplished with some type of entitlement program whereby the poor will be given money to pay for their medical bills. In addition, the government will likely force insurance companies to insure higher risk candidates, i.e., people who have pre-existing conditions.

ABORTION

It is uncertain whether any health care package will contain medical service for abortion. Pro-choice activists argue that abortion should be included, contending that exclusion would discriminate against poorer women and limit their freedom of choice. Pro-life activists argue that including abortion in a health care package would warrant state-subsidized abortion.

There have been approximately 1.6 million abortions per year since 1989. According to a 1992 report by the Centers for Disease Control, women who obtained abortions were predominantly 24 years of age or younger, white and unmarried, yet a disproportionate number of black women also receive abortions.

AIDS

The Centers for Disease Control states that from 1981 - 1992 the reported cases of AIDS were 244,939 in the U.S. In 1994 CDC estimates 1 million people are infected in the U.S. with HIV.

The U.S. Public Health Service reported July 22, 1993, that the lifetime medical cost for an AIDS patient averaged $102,000. In the U.S., the death rate for the human immunodeficiency virus infection rose to 11.3 people per 100,000 in 1991 from 9.5 in 1990.

AIDS is in a tie for 6th place among the leading causes of premature death and among these it is the fastest growing, according to the Centers for Disease Control.

Worldwide, women are becoming infected with AIDS about as often as men.

By the year 2000 most new cases will be women. The World Health Organization estimates that more than 25 million AIDS cases have occurred to 1994.

**AIDS COUNT
1994**

**1 million
infected with HIV
in U.S.**

Social State of the Nation

POVERTY AND WELFARE

For several decades, the rate of economic growth greatly reduced the poverty rate, but a combination of demographic, social, economic and policy factors has led to an increase in those falling below the poverty line. The national poverty rate of 14.2% in 1991 remains well above the levels reached in any year from 1969 through 1980.

The number of women and children below the poverty line has increased, in part because of the increase in single-mother households. Single-

Millions of People
Below the Poverty line

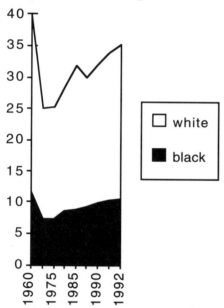

mother households have a greater chance of slipping into poverty than the traditional family or the single-father family. Nationwide, children living in poverty increased 22% in the 1980s. Children remain over represented among the poor, with a poverty rate of 21.8%.

The government offers a variety of programs for those living in poverty including welfare, food stamps and aid to families with dependent children (AFDC). Such programs cost taxpayers billions, and many argue these programs remain ineffective.

Furthermore, many say that these programs send the wrong message. Because remaining on welfare is often more profitable than working and

because families are given money based on how many children they have, the welfare system has created a dangerous cycle of dependence.

The desire to reform the welfare system has long been an objective of government. President Clinton's administration is no different. The president has suggested work-fare to replace welfare. The plan would limit the time a person could collect unemployment to two years and would force those people on welfare to work at government-funded jobs in order to receive assistance.

Cost of Welfare
in Billions of Dollars

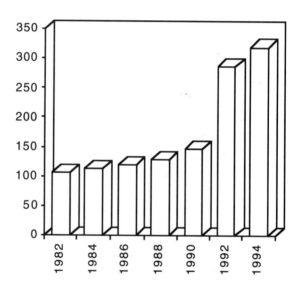

SOCIAL SECURITY

Signed into law by Franklin Roosevelt in 1935, the Social Security Program was created to ensure that the elderly would always have enough money to live on. Since that time, Social Security has become one of the most comprehensive and expensive social programs in the industrialized world. Workers and their employers each contribute an equal amount to the Social Security Program to pay for retirement, disability and Medicare benefits. Presently, Social Security deducts about 8% of earnings.

Cost of Social Security in Billions of Dollars

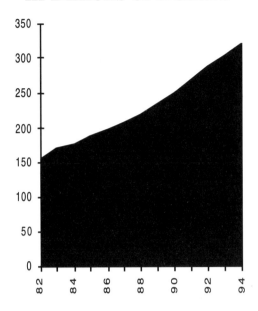

The problem with Social Security is that we have a growing number of elderly and a shrinking number of younger workers to pay for the benefits to the old. Since 1960, the number of people 65 and over has increased 89% in comparison with a 39% growth for the total population. The age group, 85 and over, has grown at a tremendous 232%.

Millions of People Over 65 in the U.S.

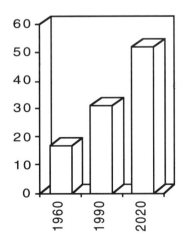

With the Baby Boomers, those born after WWII to 1964, reaching old age in the next few decades, the Social Security system faces serious problems. By the time the Baby Boomers reach retirement, there will be one worker for every three senior citizens collecting Social Security.

The government has foreseen some of these problems and has created a Social Security savings account to cover the future claims of the Baby Boomers, but the fund will likely not be enough and Social Security will continue to be America's most draining social program. Major reform is needed in Social Security, but because the elderly represent such a large percentage of the voting electorate, the system is politically untouchable.

CRIME

The United States is the most violent democracy in the world. Crime, drugs, joblessness and welfare dependency are sapping the strength of America's inner cities. Cities are struggling with crime, inadequate budgets and a disintegrating family structure.

Since 1983 the number of rapes has increased by 38%, robberies by 32%, murder by 23% and violent crimes by a staggering 54%.

Almost 66% of all murders in the United States are comitted with guns. Handguns alone account for more than half the murders. About 80% of all teenage homicides are the result of a firearm injury.

The number of Americans in jail or prison has doubled in the last eight years and has increased about 150% in the last eleven. For every 20 people in the U.S., there is one arrest.

In fiscal year 1991, the U.S. spent more than $20.1 billion on penal corrections including operations and construction, up 20% from the previous year. Still, the prisons are over-

Social State of the Nation

crowded, operating at 52% over capacity.

In 1994, after much debate, the U.S. Congress passed a crime bill which will increase funding to hire more policemen, put a ban on certain assault weapons, tighten the parole system and give money to social programs aimed at reducing crime — these include sports and educational programs. The bill was not supported by the majority of Republicans in Congress basically because of the assault weapons ban and the costs of social programs.

Number of Serious Crimes in Millions

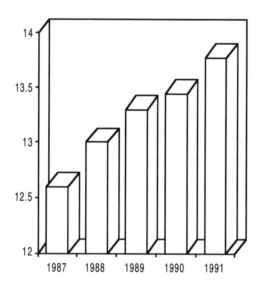

Child Abuse

In recent years, experts have declared that child abuse and neglect were epidemic. Cases of neglect have overflowed our hospitals, foster care homes, social worker case loads and court dockets. About 2.4 million cases of child abuse, child sexual abuse and child neglect are reported to child protective agencies each year. Since 1990, reports of child abuse have quadrupled. Furthermore, it is estimated that nearly two million children under age 18 are affected in some way by the substance abuse of their parents.

Drugs

A study released by the U.S. Department of Health and Human Services in 1990 estimated that drug abuse costs the U.S. $58.3 billion a year. The rate of illicit drug use remains higher for American youth than for the youth of any other industrialized country. Drug use has remained fairly constant over the past four years with slight increases in the use of LSD.

The most used drug is alcohol. A 1988 National Health Interview Survey reported that 15.3 million Americans exhibit symptoms of alcohol abuse or dependence such as binge drinking and loss of control. The economic costs of alcohol abuse were estimated to be $98.6 billion in lost productivity, deaths and treatment programs.

Another popular drug is tobacco. Approximately 400,000 people die each year because of diseases caused by smoking. Among adults, smoking has decreased but smoking among young people has remained fairly constant.

EDUCATION

More than 60 million students and approximately 7 million teachers, administrators and support staff are involved in America's public educational system. Expenditures on public elementary and secondary schools have been increasing faster than inflation and now account for 7% of GDP.

Improvements in the skill level of the U.S. labor force over this century have been dramatic. By 1990 the typical worker had completed almost 13 years of schooling and more than one-fifth of all Americans aged 25-29 had completed 4 or more years of college. These increases in education have generated returns in the form of higher wages.

Despite this good news, America still lags behind most of the industrialized countries in high school and elementary education. According to studies, U.S. children fall behind their peers in Japan, Germany, France and Korea in math, science and geography. However, at the college level U.S. students are considered equally and often better educated than their peers in other countries.

In order to reduce costs and improve the quality of our secondary education, many argue that reform is needed. Among the plans for reform are: (1) to increase competition by giving grants to

Per Pupil Spending in America's Public Schools

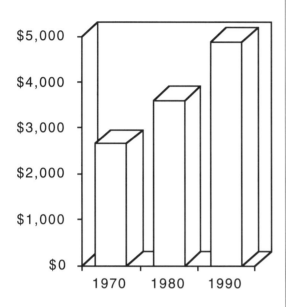

families to choose a public or private school for their children; (2) to raise standards for becoming a teacher; (3) to eliminate administration and give more power to teachers; (4) to encourage private business to help in training at school.

IMMIGRATION

Approximately half a million people immigrate to the U.S. annually and well over half of them are from two ethnic backgrounds — hispanic and asian.

The number entering the United States has increased steadily since the early 1960s — from 1.5 million in 1960-64 to 5.6 million in 1985-90. About 7.9% of the nation's population was foreign born in 1990, the highest proportion in the past four decades.

Under the current system, immigrants can gain protection from the U.S. if they prove that they are fleeing from political persecution. Although the courts are filled with immigration cases, there is evidence that the majority of immigration is

Breakdown of Immigration 1992

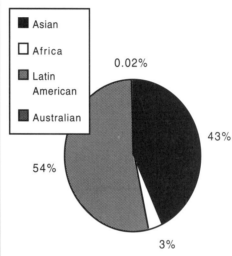

now illegal and undocumented.

Over the past several years, immigration has been at the forefront of political debate. Immigrants from China, Haiti, Cuba and Central America flee oppression in their home countries and flock to certain American cities— mainly New York, Los Angeles and Miami.

American voter sentiment is generally anti-immigration. Many argue that immigrants take jobs from U.S. workers and soak up too many government services — from education to medical care. Others argue that the U.S. has an obligation to political refugees and that immigration provides the U.S. with cultural diversity and a stronger workforce.

Reforms are underway in Washington, D.C., and we will likely see major changes in immigration policy in the future.

Top 5 States Admitting Immigrants	
States	Percent
California	34%
New York	14%
Florida	8%
Texas	8%
New Jersey	5%
Illinois	5%

HOMELESSNESS

Both policy experts and the citizenry as a whole seem to be less optimistic than they once were that the homeless problem can be eradicated. In 1987 the Urban Institute made an estimate of 500,000 to 600,000 homeless in America. The U.S. Bureau of the Census found a total of 178,828 persons in emergency shelters for the homeless and 49,793 persons visible at pre-identified street locations during a special count in 1990.

About 25% of all these homeless families are headed by women who left home to escape domestic violence. Another 50% of the homeless are single men. About 20% of the homeless are employed in full or part-time jobs and another 25% are veterans.

Many homeless are drug abusers and an even greater number are mentally ill. Leading causes of homelessness, according to a survey of mayors, are: lack of affordable housing, domestic violence, unemployment, drug abuse and teen pregnancy.

Congress appropriated approximately $1 billion last year to deal with the homeless problem, yet cities and towns continue to pay the majority of the bill. New York City reports that it spends about $500 million each year on services for the homeless.

EVENTS WITH SOCIAL IMPACT

• More Americans won the Nobel Prize than any other nationality. Winners were: **Dr. Joseph H. Taylor** and **Dr. Russel A. Hulse** in the field of physics, who won for discovering the first known binary pulsar; **Ms. Toni Morrison**, author of *The Song of Solomon, Beloved and Jazz*, literature; **Kary B. Mullis,** chemistry, for inventing a method of duplicating DNA; **Robert M. Fogel** and **Douglas C. North,** economics; **Dr. Philip A. Sharp**, for his discovery of split genes.

• Football superstar, **O.J. Simpson**, was charged with the murder of his former wife and her young acquaintance. Aside from being the one of the most interesting legal cases in history, the case also sparked questions of race and brought into light the issue of domestic abuse.

• The Midwest and South suffered the worst **flood** in over 100 years. Congress provided $6.2 billion dollars in flood relief. More than 70,000 were left homeless.

• An **Eastern storm** hit the nation in March of 1993 claiming 200 lives. The storm swept through the East Coast and the Southeastern part of the United States with as much as 36 inches of snow in some areas.

• A terrorist bomb blew up and damaged New York City's **World Trade Center,** killing 6 people.

• Senator **Robert Packwood** was charged with and apologized for behavior in the treatment of women.

• **Robert Rota**, former Postmaster of the U.S., pleaded guilty to conspiring to embezzle public funds. He admitted to giving as much as $30,000 to house members later reported to be Rep. **Dan Rostenkowski**, Democrat of Illinois, and former Rep. **Joe Kolter**, Democrat of Pennsylvania.

RESEARCH AND DEVELOPMENT (R&D)

Under the new budget, civilian Research and Development will get a $1.2 billion boost. In paving the way for the "information highway," the president is requesting $1.2 billion, a 20% increase, for research on building more sophisticated computers for use in weather forecasting and drug design in 1995. The administration is also requesting $1.8 billion for the

$11.5 billion dollars. This money will go to programs for AIDS and tuberberculosis among others.

NASA

Conversely, National Aeronautics and Space Administration's budget has received some cuts with the deepest in human space flight, building of advanced solid rocket motors for the space shuttle and research into a second-generation launch vehicle to replace the space

Spending on Research and Development in Millions of Dollars

Department or Agency	1994	1995	% Change 1994-1995
Defense	$35,538	$36,538	1.00%
National Institutes of Health	$10,845	$11,350	1.70%
NASA	$8,493	$8,597	-1.80%
Energy	$6,054	$6,052	-3.00%
National Science Foundation	$2,026	$2,220	-6.60%
Agriculture	$1,393	$1,394	-2.90%
Commerce	$985	$1,322	31.20%
Transportation	$605	$692	11.40%
Environmental Protection Agency	$533	$571	4.10%
All other	$1,824	$1,726	-8.40%
R&D Faciliticies	$2,589	$2,016	-25.00%
R&D Total	$71,073	$73,045	-0.20%

Global Change Research Program which will coordinate studies of global warming and other envionmental issues.

National Science Foundation

The National Science Foundation will receive $329 million, a 43% increase over last year. The majority of this money will go toward high performance computing and research in communications and global change. The National Institutes of Health will receive an increase of

shuttle. However, NASA did receive an increase in funding for its Mars Surveyor Program.

Department of Commerce

The Department of Commerce's technology administration is scheduled to receive a $438.4 million increase. Most of the increase will go toward the National Institute of Standards and Technology. The money will be used for high-risk, high-payoff projects, renovation and basic research.

Social State of the Nation

DEBT AND DEFICIT

Understanding the Deficit

In order to understand our economy, we must understand our journey to the present. Much of our present economic situation is a reflection of our political past. The most relevant period of history for us to understand is probably the 1980s. In some ways the 1980s were very good for the U.S. but in other ways they left us with painful legacies.

President Ronald Reagan had a very definite plan for the United States. He believed that we should have minimal government, lower taxes and lower spending. He tried to make

This release of money to the private sector, along with a deregulation of business, made the 1980s the longest period of peace-time growth.

While his tax cuts were passed in Congress, the president's spending cuts were less successful. Attempts to reduce and reform spending on Medicare, welfare and Social Security, among other entitlement programs, could not gain enough political support. The cuts that were implemented were not large enough to cover the reduction in tax revenue.

Federal Spending and Total Taxes as a Percent of GDP

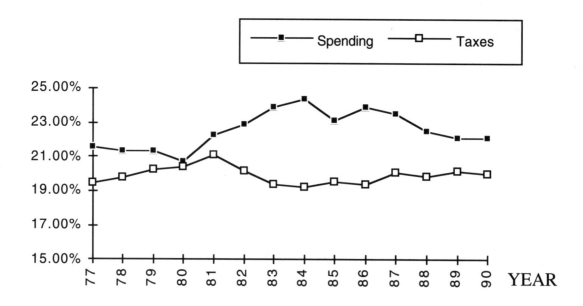

these policies a reality.

In his first years in office, President Reagan initiated some of the largest tax cuts that the U.S. has ever known. He cut both corporate income tax and personal income tax. Money which would have gone to taxes went into buying consumer goods, into investing in the stock market, into building new homes.

This situation drove a wedge between America's income and expenses. We began to spend a lot more than we were able to take in from taxes, and, thus, we created the high deficits of the 1980s.

As a result we went from the largest creditor nation of the world to the largest debtor nation.

Bankruptcy?

The first and most obvious reason the U.S. doesn't want to have debt is very obvious: bankruptcy. If we kept operating as we are today, the U.S. government would go bankrupt. It is a little hard to imagine what it would be like during a country's bankruptcy.

Bankruptcy would mean a certain amount of government shutdown -- construction in progress would halt; Social Security recipients might stop getting their checks; schools would close; inflation would probably be high. The country might look a lot like pre-WWII Germany or Russia at the end of the cold war.

Low Growth Rate

Living with constant deficits is a dangerous risk for America -- not just because of the possibility of bankruptcy. Economists also believe that our deficits are slowing our growth rate because deficits tend to draw money away from the private sector— where nearly all economic growth occurs.

In order to raise money to finance the deficit, the government must (1)tax its citizens and (2) sell government securities such as Treasury Bills. These two activities divert money from private investment into the government for its spending.

The high interest rates and the security of government bonds entice people to invest in government bonds rather than putting the money in the bank or investing in the stock market.

Because a great amount of our capital is going toward taxes and buying government bonds, there is little money left for private industry to grow and expand.

Since most government spending goes toward entitlement programs, the government does not add to the growth of the economy. The government, therefore, does not create wealth, like the private sector, but rather redistributes that wealth.

DRAWBACKS OF LIVING WITH DEFICITS AND DEBT

- **Higher Interest Rates**
- **Lower Investment**
- **Lower Growth Rate**
- **Lost Revenue to Pay Interest on Debt**
- **Being a Debtor to Foreign Countries**
- **Lower Sales of Exports**
- **Long-term Decrease in the Standard of Living**

Lost Money on Interest

Another drawback in living with debt is the fact that the U.S. has to pay interest on our debt. When the government borrows money it has to pay that money back with interest just as any individual or corporation does. The estimated interest for 1994 on our debt is 204 billion dollars — four times the amount we spend on education. This is money that could be going to public schools or to the space program or to AIDS research.

The Trade Deficit

The legacy of foreign debt is not the only cost of our foreign borrowing. To attract foreign investors to America in order to finance our debt, the U.S. had to offer higher interest rates. This in turn led to a high demand for U.S. dollars which resulted in an appreciation of the dollar. The high dollar value made it cheaper for Americans to buy

Net Exports in Billions of Dollars

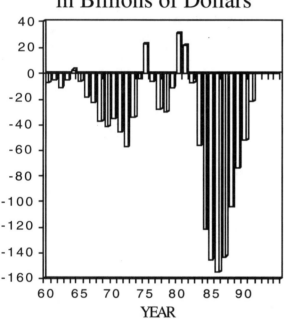

imports but harder for American exporters to sell their now relatively expensive goods abroad. Thus, throughout the 1980s American exports fell and American industry was hurt.

LOW SAVINGS RATE

Another concern of the American economy is the fact that America now has a slower growth rate than many industrialized countries. This means that the U.S. is not moving forward by producing new technology or products so fast as our competitors. Economists have studied this issue for many years and seem to believe that the reason the United States is not growing so rapidly as these other nations, such as Japan, is that America does not

save and invest its money in the future.

The U.S. saves roughly 3% of its income. Japan saves nearly 9% of its national income. Economists point to this difference in explaining the fact that Japan has a higher growth rate than the U.S.

The money that is saved in a country — that is, the money that each and every citizen puts into the bank— can be used for investment purposes. For instance, the money in a bank is loaned out to build and finance the purchase of new houses, to

Comparative Savings Rates

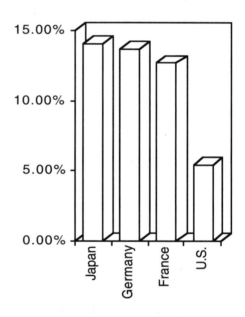

start new business ventures and build inventories.

When people don't save, there isn't any money in the bank to lend out. There is no money for the entrepreneur to start his new business and, thus, there is no new growth. This is precisely what is happening in America. We use most of our money for consumption goods —VCRs, televisions, cars, furniture — and not enough for research and education.

If we look to the example of our own families we can see the connection. Suppose we have two families, equal in all relevant aspects. Family A works very hard and puts 10% of its income in a savings account so that its child can go to college.

Family B chooses not to save its money but

30

Comparative Per Hour Earnings

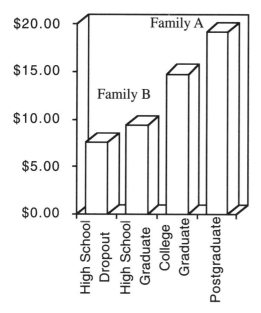

instead buys a new car, a television and a VCR, all Japanese.

The child in Family A goes to college but the child in Family B does not have enough money to pay for college. Over the course of a lifetime, Child A will be able to make a lot more money than Child B because he has a college degree. Family A decided to invest in its child's future and, thus, will be richer in the future than Family B.

We know from our own families that when we save, we are able to invest in really important things, such as our children's educations. In this way, we can make great strides in our quality of life. The fact that many Americans have not learned this lesson means that in the future we could have a lower standard of living than the Japanese. The Japanese and the Germans and many other peoples are becoming richer faster because they are saving and investing more. The U.S. is eating all of its dollars now while these countries are saving and preparing for the future.

GROWING INEQUALITY

Ever since the 1970s, inequality in income has been on the rise. Presently, we have the widest rich-poor gap since the U.S. Census Bureau began keeping track of these statistics in 1947. The top one-fifth families now earn 44.6% of all income in the U.S. compared to 4.4% of income for the bottom fifth. The national income of the richest 5% of Americans rose from 18.6% in 1977 to 24.5% in 1990 while the share for the poorest Americans fell.

There could be a variety of reasons for this increasing inequality.

(1) A less progressive tax system allowed the rich to keep more of their income and did not redistribute money to the poor.

(2) There is now a greater premium

Average Scores for 12th Graders
1992

■ Public Schools in Affluent Areas
□ Public Schools in Poor Areas

put on education. More educated workers became more highly paid while less educated were paid less.

Presently, there is less demand for blue-collar workers than in the past. Import competition and immigration have sent blue-collar jobs abroad. Furthermore, technology has made other blue-collar jobs unnecessary.

Business Week reports in August of 1994, "The well-paying blue-collar jobs that gave U.S. workers rising living standards for most of this century are vanishing. Today you can all but forget about joining the middle class unless you go to college."

Furthermore, most evidence suggests that the majority of college-bound children come from middle to upperclass families. Not suprisingly these children make higher scores on standardized tests. This means that these college-eduated children will likely remain in the upper class while the children of the poor who do not attend college will likely remain poor because of their lack of education.

GROWING GAP BETWEEN THE RICH AND THE POOR

Income Level	Average Family Income as Share of National Income		Average Family Income		% Change
	1980	**1992**	**1980**	**1992**	
Top 25%	48.2%	51.3%	$78,844	$91,368	up 15.9%
Second 25%	26.9%	26.3%	$44,041	$46,471	up 5.5%
Third 25%	17.3%	16.0%	$28,249	$28,434	up 0.7%
Bottom 25%	7.6%	6.5%	$12,359	$11,530	down 6.8%

SLOW RECOVERY

During the past several years, the economy has experienced a slowdown in economic growth beginning in 1989 and reaching a peak with the recession of late 1990 and early 1991. An unusually weak recovery came in March 1991.

During 1992, the U.S. economy remained in a modest and uneven recovery with the rate of growth picking up to the 2.5 to 3% range.

Economists point to several reasons for the slow recovery from the recession. First was the downsizing of the military. The large cuts in defense spending created much unemployment. Second, just as the U.S. was recovering from the recession, Japan, Germany and many other countries were just beginning their recessions. Because the U.S. trades so heavily with these countries, the U.S. export market was hurt.

Finally, the fact that America has such high debt created a credit crunch. Large government deficits that were taking money from the private sector, coupled with overly tight regulation on bank lending — because of the fear of another savings and loan crisis — contributed to the fact that businesses could not find money to expand.

SIGNS OF IMPROVEMENT

Although growth was sluggish in 1993, the economy is now beginning to make some headway. By the latter part of 1993, the economy was said to have grown by about 6% (annual rate). Demand and final sales increased. Furthermore, there seemed to be improvements in labor productivity.

Consumers have trimmed their installment debt and have taken advantage of low interest rates to refinance their mortgages. Low interest rates have helped households and businesses reduce the cost of paying off existing debt. Low mortgage rates helped to make housing more afford able in the 1990s than it had been at any time in the past 18 years and created a burst of refinancing activity.

Corporations have been raising equity, on balance, for the first time in several years. America is once again the world's leading exporter and is more internationally competitive than it has been in many years.

LOW INFLATION

During 1992, inflation fell to the lowest rate in a generation. Slow money growth over the past several years contributed to, as well as reflected, the sluggish economy and waning inflationary pressures. Inflation is expected to remain low in the coming years not only because of the excess capacity of resources in the immediate future but also because of the Federal Reserve's ongoing efforts to keep inflation in check.

Low inflation not only benefits the economy but helps set the stage for sustained economic expansion. Low inflation also helps to maintain the purchasing power of Americans' savings and wealth.

UNEMPLOYMENT FALLS

The unemployment rate is the number of people who cannot find work divided by the total labor force. The unemployment rate helps to measure whether the economy is operating at full potential, that is if we are using all our labor.

The unemployment rate, although it was high during the recession of 1990 and 1991, is expected to show steady but gradual decline reaching a level of 5.3% by 1997.

An increase in labor productiv-

ity is expected to continue as the economy settles into a sustained expansion and higher investment boosts the stock of productive capital.

TAXES

President Clinton's new tax bill raised tax rates on the wealthier members of society. He also reduced certain tax deductions in an attempt to reduce the deficit.

The good news is that our tax burden still remains less than that of many countries in Latin America and the European Community, although our tax burden is higher than many Asian countries.

Probably the biggest problem

Compartive Tax Burden as a Percent of GNP

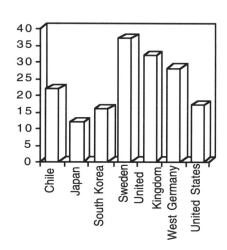

with our tax system is the fact that it distorts taxpayers' choices about how to consume, save and invest. The present income tax misallocates capital across the economy because income earned by different assets is taxed at different rates.

Moreover, the current system taxes interest on savings, dividends and capital gains, creating double taxation. As a result, taxes create a bias against investment, favoring current consumption over future consumption. This is a problem because it encourages people not to save and thus inhibits our growth potential.

AMERICA'S PLACE IN THE NEW WORLD ORDER

Ethnic Wars and Civil Unrest

Ever since the end of the Cold War in the late '80s, America has been struggling to redefine its foreign policy. The old order of the bipolar world which kept ethnic tensions in check for so many years no longer exists. The globe is torn by ethnic wars and civil unrest: Bosnia, Somalia, Rwanda, the Middle East, Haiti and throughout the former Soviet Republics. As 1994 ends, there are more than three dozen trouble spots around the globe — either now in open conflict or ready to fight at the slightest provocation.

Amidst the turmoil, America debates how to react. Should America remain the protector of human rights and freedom for the world? And if we should, what groups should we support in the various civil wars that are raging all over the globe? Should we merely send troops to keep the peace as we did in Somalia? Should we allow our troops to attack as we did in the Gulf War? If we do engage, will the American people be willing to give up not only valuable resources that could be used domestically but also the lives of our soldiers?

A Confusing Foreign Policy

As it stands now, America has no clear foreign policy. It seems that we are reacting to events as they arise in no certain pattern. Most experts agree that this kind of reactionary foreign policy is dangerous.

Our actions in Bosnia, Somalia, Haiti and Cuba have been confusing and ineffective. In Bosnia, Serbians continue to target civilian areas and have failed to uphold agreements to honor 'safe-haven zones' or to remove some of their larger weapons. In Somalia, our troops were fired on and were ineffective in bringing any comprehensive help to starving areas.

In the Caribbean in recent months we have also experienced failure. In Haiti, our embargo has failed to oust the military coup leaders. Because our troops were not allowed to fire, our peace-keeping forces could not land on the island as they were fired on by the Haitian military. Finally, in Cuba our long-standing reluctance to recognize Castro has not driven him from office. In an attempt to fight back, Castro seems to be generating another "Mariel Boat Lift" of Cuban exiles into South Florida.

One of the facts that makes taking any strong military action difficult is that these lesser developed nations have access to sophisticated weapons -- mainly because our defense contractors are selling them weapons. While there have been a number of improvements concerning the ban of weapons, trading in weapons is still a very profitable market. Not surprisingly, the U.S. has been the major supplier of arms to the Third World. In 1992, the U.S. accounted for more than half of all arms transfers to the Third World.

In order to deal effectively with the new kind of challenges that appear in our world, most military and foreign policy leaders agree that we need a clear, cohesive plan. As a people, we must demand that our leaders develop a structured and strong foreign policy for the defense of our nation.

Arms Transfers to the Third World

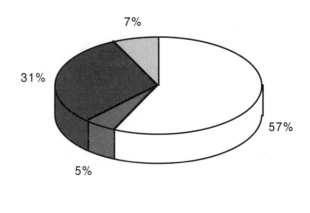

7%
31%
5%
57%

☐ United States ▨ Russia ■ Western Europe ▨ All Others

As former Secretary of Defense Casper Weinberger points out, "The only effective way to avoid war is to demonstrate credibly that one is strong enough, resolved enough and prepared enough to go to war." It is foolish to believe that just because the Cold War is over America is safe. Indeed, we may be in greater peril than ever before. Judging from an upsurge in terrorism such as the World Trade Center bombing, the new terrorist training camps in Afghanistan and the sale of nuclear and conventional weaponry by the former Soviet Republics and by America itself, the world sees an America that still has much to battle.

A New Kind of Military

To meet the challenges of the New World Order, America must redirect its military to deal with ethnic and civil wars. Since the end of the Cold War, the U.S. military has tried to transform itself from an entity capable of conducting a complete nuclear war against the communist world to an entity able to launch small, fast, conventional units for peace keeping in distant lands. We must be ready for a variety of different terrains and a variety of different conflicts. In a world where conflict could spring up anywhere, our greatest weakness is not knowing our enemy.

Furthermore, as many military strategists point out, coming wars will be wars of technology. In the future, our enemies may introduce viruses into our computers rather than launching bombs on our shores. They may genetically engineer diseases or intercept our communications with satellites. These are the kinds of attacks that America must be capable of combating.

A military projection game played by the Military Academies pits America against China decades into the future. China wins because she is able to muster the technological know-how to win the space-age war. Such futuristic exercises

Weapons Ban

• After 24 years of negotiating with more than 120 countries, the U.S. signed a **chemical weapons ban**. Countries are given 10 years to destroy any existing stockpiles of chemical weapons. The only country refusing to sign the agreement was Iraq.

• The United States and Russia agreed to reduce their strategic **nuclear arms** by two-thirds.

• After some tense moments, North Korea promised to give up its **nuclear weapon production** in exchange for some economic and technological help from the U.S. and South Korea.

indicate that America's defense program is lacking.

Amidst a need for transformation, the military has had to deal with large budget cuts. By 1997, defense will suffer reductions greater than 40 billion dollars. Furthermore, 130 military bases are scheduled to close and another 45 bases are scheduled for scaling down. The star wars defense plan was abandoned by the defense department in order to reduce the size of the defense budget. Thirty billion dollars had already been spent previously on research.

Defense Spending in Billions of Dollars

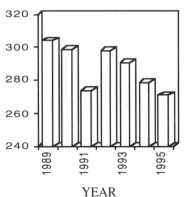

YEAR

INTERNATIONAL TRADE

Trade has become an ever more important sector of the U.S. economy. Presently, the U.S. has a trade deficit. This means that we import more than we export. In other words, we buy more foreign products than foreigners buy American goods. There could be several reasons for this:

(1) Some countries, such as Japan, have high trade barriers making it difficult for the U.S. to sell products there.

(2) The U.S. dollar has been high compared to other currencies making it expensive for foreigners to buy American and inexpensive for Americans to buy foreign.

(3) U.S. products are less competitive than foreign products.

America's Trade Deficit or Surplus with the Rest of the World 1992	
Austrialia	5.8 billion
Western Europe	17.1
Canada	-19.8
Japan	-50.5
OPEC	-13.0
Eastern Europe	3.6
Other	35.6

Free Trade

Over the past several decades, the world has become more interdependent economically. Between 1965 and 1990, inflation-adjusted merchandise exports grew by 439%, while world production rose 136%. As trade becomes more important to their economies, nations try to promote free trade by encouraging the peoples they trade with most to lower their tariffs (or taxes on foreign goods). During the past several years, we have seen the development of free trade zones in Europe (EC), North America (NAFTA), South America (Mercosur and the Andean Pact) and Asia (APEC).

Nearly all economists agree that free trade brings great benefits to all. Free trade offers consumers the greatest number of choices at the best prices. The philosophy is that we can all benefit from each other's strengths. If, for instance, the Japanese make better radios and the U.S. makes better refrigerators, then it benefits both countries to trade what they do best. In this way, American citizens can buy great radios and the Japanese can purchase great refrigerators and both countries are better off than if they had not traded.

It is this gradual realization that trade benefits all concerned that has driven America and most other countries to work toward free trade. This is not an easy goal. While free trade benefits

America's Trading Partners
1992

U.S. Exports

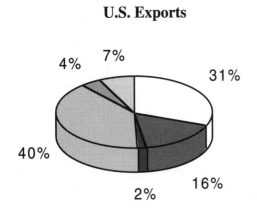

U.S. Imports

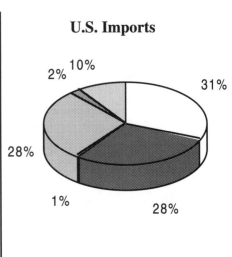

- ☐ Canada
- ■ Japan
- ■ Eastern Europe
- ▨ Western Europe
- ▨ Austrailia, New Zealand, South Africa
- ☐ OPEC

everyone in the long run, it is sometimes difficult for a nation to make the transition to free trade. This is because free trade often forces a nation to restructure its economy.

Going back to our example of the U.S. and the Japanese, we might observe that when the U.S. begins to trade with Japan, the U.S. radio manufacturers are hurt by trade because people buy Japanese radios rather than American. Gradually, U.S. citizens unemployed by the radio industry have to find new jobs — for instance, the new jobs created by the refrigerator industry. While this process of restructuring can be a painful one for society, it yields great benefits by forcing the country to produce more efficiently, making the whole society richer in the long run.

WHAT FREE TRADE WILL YIELD FOR AMERICA

The Uruguay Round of GATT
$100 billion annually from increased exports and cheaper imports by 2005.

NAFTA
200,000 new jobs from increased demand for U.S. exports within 15 years.

GATT

The General Agreement on Tariffs and Trade (GATT) was established in January 1948 to reduce tariffs and to promote free trade. Eighty-seven signatory countries and an additional 27 countries belong to GATT. Together they account for 85% of all world trade.

The latest set of negotiations in the General Agreement on Tariffs and Trade (GATT), the Uruguay Round, was completed in 1994. The agreement called for the lowering of tariff and non-tariff

barriers in a variety of different areas including agriculture. It also attempted to address complicated issues such as intellectual property rights. The agreement is said to add about $300 billion to the world product in increased productivity.

NAFTA

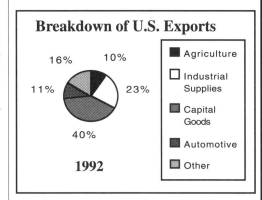

Breakdown of U.S. Exports

16% 10%
11% 23%
40%

1992

Agriculture
Industrial Supplies
Capital Goods
Automotive
Other

By a close vote, the North American Free Trade Agreement was passed by Congress. Over a period of 15 years, NAFTA will eliminate most trade barriers among Canada, Mexico and the U.S., making the three countries a free trade zone. The treaty creates a free trade area of 370 million consumers and more than $6.5 trillion of annual output, linking the U.S. to our largest trading partner, Canada, and third largest trading partner, Mexico.

The main arguments against NAFTA were that (1) Americans would lose their jobs to cheaper foreign labor and (2) environmental standards of Mexico were not up to American or Canadian standards. To correct these problems, NAFTA (1) created funds to support and retrain those who might lose their jobs to Mexican or Canadian workers. In addition, NAFTA is to be implemented slowly giving people time to adjust and (2) NAFTA forced Mexico to comply with stricter environmental standards.

THE ENVIRONMENT

Global Warming and the Depletion of Ozone

Scientists believe that at the current rate the earth is likely to warm by as much as 3° to 5°F over the next 50 years. This warming could set off a chain of events beginning with the melting of the polar ice caps, a rise in the sea level, flooding and the eventual destruction of much coastal land.

Risks According to the Environmental Protection Agency

High Risk	Habitat Destruction Global Warming Ozone Layer Depletion Species Extinction Biological Diversity
Medium Risk	Pesticides Surface Water Pollution Air Pollution
Low Risk	Oil Spills Radioactive Materials Groundwater Pollution

Global warming is occurring because sunlight is trapped inside the earth's atmosphere by toxic gases that emanate from our industries, cars and other man-made products. This is most commonly known as the greenhouse effect.

Greenhouse gases include chlorfluorocarbons (CFCs), methane and nitrous oxide. The worst gases are the CFCs because they also destroy the ozone layer which protects the earth from the sun's ultraviolet rays.

In this decade, delegates from 87 nations met in Copenhagen and together they agreed to increase the schedules for phasing out chemicals that damage the earth's ozone layer. Under the agreement, some chemicals would be regulated for the first time. Chloraphorbins, the chemicals thought to be the most harmful to the ozone, will be phased out by 1996. CFCs have been traditionally used in air-conditioning, cleaning, insulation and as aerosol propellants.

Deforestation and Loss of Biodiversity

The great majority of deforestation today occurs in the tropical rain forests located in Central and South America, equatorial Africa, Southeast Asia and Northeastern Australia. It is estimated that the world may be losing more than 49 million acres of tropical rainforest each year.

With the loss of forest comes the loss of biodiversity. In a four-mile radius, a typical patch of rain forest contains 750 species of trees, 750 species of other plants, 125 species of mammals, 400 species of birds, 100 species of reptiles and 60 species of amphibians. The destruction of all of this life has dire consequences for the human race. For example, of the 3,000 plant species that help fight cancer 70% are located in the rain forest.

Destruction of Wetlands

Wetlands regulate water flows by storing water and buffering the effects of storms, purifying and filtering water and providing a habitat for a wide variety of plants and animals.

Over the past several decades, though, wetlands have been drained, cleared, exploited and built on. It is estimated that America has more than half of its original wetlands. This loss has resulted in the pollution of fresh water, loss of species and erosion of land.

Superfund

In 1980 Congress created the Superfund which provides $1.6 billion for the cleanup of thousands of hazardous waste sights, but there have been many complaints about the Superfund. In its history, it has only cleaned 84 high priority sites and of the $1.3 billion spent thus far, $1 billion has gone toward legal fees.

CONTENTS

"Each year, you work to May 3
just to pay your taxes.

Looking at it another way, you
work 2 hours and 41 minutes
in your eight-hour day
for the government."

Financial Review

Tax Freedom Day

To measure the total tax burden on individual taxpayers, experts have devised a formula to calculate how much you have to work to pay all your taxes. If you began paying your taxes January 1 with your salary and spent no money until taxes were paid off, the day you started paying for your personal necessities is called Tax Freedom Day. In 1929, the beginning of the Great Depression, tax freedom day was Feb. 9; in 1993, it was May 3. Looked at another way, while you would have spent 52 minutes out of each eight-hour day to earn enough money for a day's worth of taxes in 1929, you now spend 2 hours and 41 minutes. In other words, you spend 3.10 times more of your annual income on taxes now than you would have 60 years ago.

TAX FREEDOM DAY

Year	Tax Freedom Day [1]	Tax bite in the eight-hour day [2]		
		Total	Federal	State/Local
1929	Feb. 9	0:52	0:19	0:33
1940	Mar. 8	1:29	0:45	0:44
1950	Apr. 3	2:02	1:30	0:32
1960	Apr. 16	2:20	1:40	0:40
1970	Apr. 26	2:32	1:40	0:52
1980	May 1	2:40	1:48	0:52
1985	May 1	2:38	1:44	0:54
1990	May 3	2:41	1:45	0:56
1991	May 2	2:41	1:45	0:56
1992	May 3	2:40	1:42	0:58
1993	May 3	2:41	1:43	0:58

1. The date on which the average person would finish paying federal, state and local taxes if all earnings since January 1 were turned over to government to fulfill annual tax obligations. 2. Reflects the amount of time out of each workday that the average person spends earning enough money to pay tax obligations. Source: Universal Almanac, 1994.

The financial review will explain the process by which the government taxes its citizens and then in turn spends the money it collects. While some of the information is similar to financial highlights, the financial review is a more in-depth explanation of the processes and finances of our federal government.

Section One: The Budget and Its Process

• The Expanded Budget gives a more in depth look at the government's receipts and outlays. Unlike the more concise budget offered in financial highlights, the expanded budget goes over the funds appropriated to the individual departments in government, such as the State Department or the Interior Department. In addition, it also indicates the money that goes toward different government programs such as the Food Stamps Program or the Farmer's Home Administration Program.

• The total amount taken in through taxes and other receipts was approximately $1.1 trillion in 1992. The amount spent by the government was approximately $1.4 trillion in 1992. This in turn means that our deficit for 1992 was approximately $.3 trillion.

• Next is a list of the Civilian Employment of the United States and their payrolls. This tells you khow many people the federal government employs and what their salaries are.

• In addition, a Federal Budget Schedule is included. This explains how and when the components of the Federal Budget are decided upon. Congress will receive the president's proposed budget on the 1st Monday after January 3. After that date, the Congress will debate the budget. The final budget must be passed before the beginning of the new fiscal year which begins on October 1. In order to lobby your Congressmen about the budget, you must do so after the first of January and before the first of October.

Section Two: Debt Ownership

This one page of tables shows how America finances its debt. The government sells securities such as U.S. Treasury Bills and Bonds in order to pay for its debt (ie., the accumulation of deficit). These securities have a variety of different maturities and are owned by a variety of different agents — citizens, foreigners, corporations, pension funds, etc. The majority of debt is owned by our own citizens — roughly 80%.

Section Three: Taxes

In order to get money to pay for all its functions, the government taxes its citizens. The chart entitled Cost of Collecting Federal Taxes and Collections by Principal Sources shows how the U.S. collects its taxes. The majority of taxes comes from income and profit — either from an individual or a corporation. The second most important tax is the employment tax, ie., the Social Security tax.

In 1992, the government collected $1.1 trillion dollars. The average tax "per capita" or per person in the U.S. was $4,375. If, however, we exclude non-workers from our calculation — like children — we find that the average federal tax bill per worker in the U.S. was just over $10,000.

The table labeled Federal Income Tax Comparisons gives an example of the amount of taxes that we had to pay for selected years. For instance, if you were single and had an income of $30,000 you probably paid about $3,833 in federal taxes. Federal Income taxes are progressive. This means that the higher income you have, the greater a percentage of that income you have to pay to the federal government. Since 1975, taxes have decreased because the large tax cuts of the 1980s under President Reagan.

In addition, the individual corporate income tax schedules are included. These give rough estimates of what tax rate you will have to pay depending on the income that you or your company brings in. Again, we can see that the tax system is progressive.

On the opposite page, we see a listing of Who Must File for taxes and also a list of the major changes in our federal tax methods. Together these changes are known as the Omnibus Budget Reconciliation Act of 1993 or OBRA 93.

This and more information is available to us through the Internal Revenue Service. As taxpayers, we have the rights guaranteed to us by the Taxpayer Bill of Rights to demand to know everything about how we are taxed and where our tax money goes.

THE FEDERAL BUDGET — The following gives a more in-depth budget than the financial highlights. Receipts are all the money the government takes in through taxes. Outlays are all the money the government spends either in service or transfer type payments.

U. S. Budget Receipts and Outlays — 1989-1992 (in billions)

Classification:	Fiscal 1989	Fiscal 1990	Fiscal 1991	Fiscal 1992
NET RECEIPTS				
Individual income taxes	**$445,690**	**$466,884**	**$467,827**	**$476,465**
Corporation income taxes	**$103,291**	**$93,507**	**$98,086**	**$100,270**
Social insurance taxes and contributions:				
Federal old age and survivors insurance	$240,595	$255,031	$265,503	$273,137
Federal disability insurance	$23,071	$26,625	$28,382	$29,289
Federal hospital insurance	$65,396	$68,556	$72,842	$79,109
Railroad retirement fund	$3,798	$3,679	$3,799	$3,957
Total employment taxes and contributions	**$332,860**	**$353,891**	**$370,526**	**$385,492**
Other insurance and retirem't.				
Unemployment	$22,011	$21,635	$20,922	$23,410
Federal employees retirem't	$4,428	$4,405	$4,459	$4,683
Non-federal employees	$119	$117	$108	$105
Total social insurance taxes and contributions	**$359,418**	**$380,048**	**$396,015**	**$413,690**
Excise Taxes	$34,386	$35,345	$42,402	$45,570
Estate and gift taxes	$8,745	$11,500	$11,138	$11,143
Customs duties	$16,334	$16,607	$15,949	$17,359
Deposits of earnings —				
Federal Reserve Banks	$19,604	$24,319	$19,158	$22,920
All other miscellaneous receipts	$3,233	$3,101	$3,686	$4,275
Net Budget Receipts	**$990,703**	**$1,031,204**	**$1,054,263**	**$1,091,692**
NET OUTLAYS				
Legislative Branch	$2,095	$2,244	$2,296	$2,677
The Judiciary	$1,492	$1,641	$1,989	$2,295
Executive Office of the President:				
The White House Office	$27	$30	$32	$36
Office of Mgmt. & Budget	$42	$44	$53	$54
Total Executive Office	**$124**	**$157**	**$193**	**$190**
Funds approriated to the President:				
International security assistance	$1,012	$8,352	$9,531	$7,203
Multinational assistance	$1,492	$1,695	$1,520	$1,717
Agency for International Dvlpt.	$1,215	$1,773	$1,835	$2,142
International Dvlpt. Assistance	$2,780	$3,528	$3,444	$4,029
Total funds appropriated to the President	**$4,257**	**$10,086**	**$11,724**	**$11,108**
Agriculture Department:				
Food stamp program	$13,725	$15,923	$19,649	$22,800
Farmer's Home Admin.	$7,608	$6,713	$6,629	$4,455
Forest service	$2,944	$2,934	$3,001	$3,293
Total Agriculture Department	**$48,316**	**$46,012**	**$54,119**	**$56,436**
Commerce Department:				
Total Commerce Department	**$2,571**	**$3,734**	**$2,585**	**$2,567**
Bureau of the Census	$557	$1,575	$451	$302
Defense Department:				
Military personnel	$80,676	$75,622	$83,439	$81,171
Operation and maintenance	$87,001	$88,340	$101,769	$92,042
Procurement	$81,620	$80,972	$82,028	$74,881
Research, dvlpt., test, evaluation	$37,002	$37,458	$34,589	$34,632
Military construction	$5,275	$5,080	$3,497	$4,262
Total Defense Dept.(Military)	**$294,881**	**$289,755**	**$261,925**	**$286,632**
Defense Department (civil)	$23,450	$24,975	$26,543	$28,265

U. S. Budget Receipts and Outlays — 1989-1992, cont'd:

Classification:	Fiscal 1989	Fiscal 1990	Fiscal 1991	Fiscal 1992
NET OUTLAYS (cont'd.)				
Education Department	$21,608	$23,109	$25,339	$26,047
Energy Department	$11,387	$12,023	$12,459	$15,439
Health & Human Services Dept.:				
Food and Drug Administration	$510	$553	$648	$752
National Institutes of Health	$6,992	$7,492	$7,677	$8,376
Public Health Service	$12,250	$14,007	$15,348	$17,447
Health Care Financing Adm.	$163,028	$184,893	$205,776	$239,366
Total Health/Human Svcs. Dept.	**$172,301**	**$193,679**	**$217,969**	**$257,961**
Social Security (Off Budget)	$227,473	$244,998	$266,395	$281,418
Housing and Urban Dvlpt. Dept.	$19,680	$20,167	$22,751	$24,470
Interior Department	$5,308	$5,795	$6,095	$6,555
Justice Department:				
Federal Bureau of Investigation	$1,528	$1,473	$1,695	$1,832
Total Justice Department	**$6,232**	**$6,507**	**$8,244**	**$9,826**
Labor Department:				
Unemployment Trust Fund	$18,730	$20,250	$28,434	$41,294
Total Labor Department	**$22,657**	**$25,316**	**$34,040**	**$47,193**
State Department	$3,722	$3,979	$4,252	$5,007
Transportation Department:				
Federal Aviation Adm.	$5,740	$6,391	$7,241	$8,155
Total Transportation Dept.	**$26,607**	**$28,637**	**$30,503**	**$32,560**
Treasury Department:				
Internal Revenue Service	$11,049	$12,053	$13,689	$17,904
Interest on the public debt	$240,863	$264,853	$285,472	$292,330
Total Treasury Department	**$230,566**	**$255,264**	**$276,352**	**$293,428**
Veterans Affairs Department	$30,041	$28,998	$31,214	$33,737
Environmental Protection Agency	$4,906	$5,108	$5,770	$5,932
General Services Administration	-$462	-$123	$487	$469
Nat. Aeronautics/Space Admin.	$11,036	$12,429	$13,878	$13,961
Office of the Personnel Mgmt.	$29,073	$31,949	$34,808	$35,596
Small Business Administration	$85	$692	$613	$394
Selected independent agencies:				
Action	$163	$169	$192	$194
Board for Int'l. Broadcasting	$199	$208	$228	$210
Corporation for Public Broadcasting	$228	$229	$299	$327
District of Columbia	$538	$578	$671	$691
Equal Employment Opportunity Commission	$182	$181	$192	$209
Export-Import Bank of the U.S.	$47	$357	-$88	-$119
Federal Communication Comm.	$49	$79	$66	$78
Federal Deposit Insurance Corp.	$2,847	$6,429	$7,363	$3,666
Federal Trade Commission	$65	$57	$60	$71
Interstate Commerce Comm.	$44	$43	$45	$40
Legal Services Corporation	$309	$291	$344	$329
Nat. Archives & Record Adm.	$71	$157	$172	$226
Nat. Foundation on the Arts and Humanities	$309	$307	$325	$331
Nat. Labor Relations Board	$136	$141	$143	$155
National Science Foundation	$1,752	$1,838	$2,081	$2,249
Nuclear Regulatory Comm.	$189	$221	-$1	$50
Railroad Retirement Board	$4,315	$4,477	$4,358	$4,843
Securities & Exchange Comm.	$140	$129	$143	$117
Smithsonian Institution	$288	$302	$340	$378
Tennessee Valley Authority	$348	-$312	$740	$1,469
U. S. Information Agency	$888	$888	$1,001	$1,050
Total independent agencies	**$33,770**	**$73,666**	**$81,217**	**$81,876**
Undistributed offsetting receipts	-$89,155	-$99,025	-$110,005	-$117,118
Net Budget Outlays	**$1,144,020**	**$1,251,776**	**$1,323,757**	**$1,381,895**
Less net receipts	$990,701	$1,031,308	$1,054,265	$1,091,692
Deficit	**-$153,319**	**-$220,468**	**-$269,492**	**-$290,203**

1993 Annual Salaries of Federal Officials:

President of the U. S.	$200,000 [1]
Senators and Representatives	$133,000
Vice President of the U. S.	$171,500 [2]
President Pro Tempore of Senate	$148,000
Cabinet Members	$148,400
Majority & Minority Leader of the Senate	$148,400
Deputy Secretaries of State, Defense, Treasury	$133,600
Majority & Minority Leader of the House	$148,400
Deputy Attorney General	$133,600
Speaker of the House	$171,500
Secretaries of the Army, Navy, Air Force	$133,600
Chief Justice of the United States	$171,500
Under Secretaries of executive departments	$123,100
Associate Justices of the Supreme Court	$164,100

(1) Plus taxable $50,000 for expenses and a nontaxable sum [not to exceed $100,000 a year] for travel expenses. (2) Plus taxable $10,000 for expenses.

<u>NOTE</u>: *All salaries shown above are taxable. (Source: Office of Personnel Management).*

Civilian Employment of the Federal Government in May 1993

Source: Workforce Analysis and Statistics Division. U. S. Office of Personnel Management.
(Payroll in thousands of dollars for the month of May 1993).

Agency	ALL AREAS Employment	Payroll
Total, all agencies[1]	**3,033,215**	**$10,323,268**
Legislative Branch	**38,779**	**157,762**
Congress	20,695	66,417
U. S. Senate	7,723	24,698
House of Rep. Summary	12,954	41,633
Comm. on Scty. & Coop in Eur.	18	86
Architect of the Capitol	2,334	9,238
Botanic Garden	51	216
Competit Policy Council	6	28
Congressional Budget Office	239	1,631
Copyright Royalty Tribunal	8	65
General Accounting Office	5109	31,747
Government Printing Office	4,775	22,350
John C. Stennis Ctr. Pub. Dev.	6	16
Library of Congress	4,999	23,358
Nat. Comm. on AIDS Syndrome	11	44
Nat. Comm. Prev. Infant Mort.	10	27
Office Technology Assessment	217	1,301
U. S. Tax Court	319	1,324
Judicial Branch	**28,075**	**133,183**
Supreme Court	371	1,094
U. S. Courts	27,618	131,639
U. S. Court of Vets. Appeals	86	450
Executive Branch	**2,966,361**	**10,032,323**
Exec. Ofc. of the President	1,991	7,598
White House Office	559	1,798
Ofc. of Vice President	23	105
Ofc. of Mgmt. & Budget	564	2,456
Office of Administration	241	715
Council Economic Advisors	33	133
Council on Environ. Qual.	23	83
Office of Policy Development	52	190
Executive Residence at White House	93	581
National Crit. Materials Council	2	8
National Security Council	65	240
National Space Council	7	5
Office of National Drug Control	90	351
Office of Science & Technology Policy	39	110
Office of U. S. Trade Rep.	200	823

Executive Departments	**2,001,621**	**6,968,252**
State	26,220	153,086
Treasury	165,530	743,467
Defense, Total	941,608	2,731,443
Department of the Army	306,562	827,905
Army, Military Func. Total	275,857	751,411
Army, Civil Func. Total	30,705	76,494
Corps of Engineers	30,565	76,170
Cemeterial Expenses	140	324
Department of the Navy	285,079	898,000
Department of the Air Force	196,074	557,131
Defense Log Agency	64,120	178,758
Other Defense Activities	89,773	269,649
Justice	98,022	463,622
Interior	84,736	335,269
Agriculture	123,057	464,622
Commerce	38,651	177,589
Labor	17,609	88,358
Health and Human Services	132,406	585,517
Housing and Urban Development	13,208	65,684
Transportation	69,922	302,919
Energy	20,637	124,146
Education	5,001	26,508
Veterans Affairs	265,014	706,022
Independent Agencies[1]	**962,749**	**3,056,473**
Action	418	2,196
Environmental Protection Agency	18,478	98,110
Equal Employment Opp. Comm.	2,938	14,475
Federal Deposit Ins. Corp.	21,889	123,339
Federal Emergency Mgmt. Agency	4,117	18,265
General Services Admin.	20,780	95,503
National Archives & Recds. Admin.	3,133	9,270
National Aero Space Admin.	25,149	148,159
Nuclear Regulatory Comm.	3,542	17,195
Office of Personnel Mgmt.	6,842	24,985
Panama Canal Commission	8,495	27,934
Securities & Exchange Commission	2,697	16,381
Small Business Admin.	5,363	25,461
Smithsonian, Summary	5,491	22,862
Tennessee Valley Authority	19,145	75,470
U. S. Information Agency	8,298	33,960
U. S. Int'l. Dev. Coop. Agency	4,385	26,413
U. S. Postal Service	779,606	2,166,456

(1) Included in total are other independent agencies with fewer than 2,500 employees.

THE FEDERAL BUDGET PROCESS

The schedule listed below shows the steps and the time frames that the government goes through in order to create our nation's budget.

Source: Executive Office of the President, Office of Management and Budget and The World Alamanac and Book of Facts 1994.

CBO = Congressional Budget Office   GRH = Gramm-Rudham-Hollings (Balanced Budget and Emergency Deficit Control Act of 1985)   OMB = Office of Management and Budget.

EXECUTIVE BUDGET PROCESS	TIMING	CONGRESSIONAL BUDGET PROCESS
Agencies subject to executive branch review submit initial budget request materials.	Sept. 1	
Fiscal year begins: President's initial GRH sequester order take effect (amounts are withheld from obligation pending issuance of final order).	Oct. 1	Fiscal year begins.
	Oct. 10	CBO issues revised GRH report to OMB and Congress.
OMB reports on changes in initial GRH estimates and determinations resulting from legislation enacted and regulations promulgated after its initial report to Congress. President issues final GRH sequester order, effective immediately, and transmits message to Congress within 15 days of final order. Agencies not subject to executive branch review submit budget request materials.	Oct. 15	
	Nov. 15	Comptroller General issues GRH compliance report.
Legislative Branch and the judiciary submit budget request materials.	Nov.-Dec.	
President transmits budget to Congress.	1st Mon. after Jan. 3	Congress receives the President's budget.
OMB sends allowance letters to agencies.	Jan.-Feb.	
	Feb. 15	CBO reports to the Budget Committees on the President's budget.
	Feb. 25	Committees submit views and estimates to Budget Committee in their own house.
OMB and the President conduct reviews to establish presidential policy to guide agencies in developing the next budget.	Apr.-June	
	Apr. 1	Senate Budget Committee reports concurrent resolution on the budget.
	Apr. 15	Congress completes action on concurrent resolution.
	May 15	House may consider appropriations bills in the absence of a concurrent resolution on the budget.
	June 10	House Appropriations Committee reports last appropriations bill.
	June 15	Congress completes action on reconciliation legislation.
	June 30	House completes action on annual appropriations bills.
President transmits the mid-session review, updating the budget estimates.	July 15	Congress receives mid-session review of the budget.
OMB provides agencies with policy guidance for the upcoming budget.	July-Aug.	
Date of "snapshot" of projected deficits for the upcoming fiscal year for initial OMB and CBO GRH reports.	Aug. 15	
	Aug. 20	CBO issues its initial GRH report to OMB and Congress.
OMB issues its initial GRH report providing estimates and determinations to the President and Congress.	Aug. 25	
President issues initial GRH sequester order and sends message to Congress within 15 days.		

Public Debt of the U.S. *(Source: Bureau of Public Debt, U.S. Department of Treasury and The World Almanac and Book of Facts, 1994).*

Fiscal Year	*Debt (billions)*	*Per. cap. (dollars)*	*Interest paid (billions)*	*% of federal outlays*
1977	$698.8	$3,170	$41.9	10.2
1978	771.5	3,463	48.7	10.6
1979	826.5	3,669	59.8	11.9
1980	907.7	3,985	74.9	12.7
1981	997.9	4,338	95.6	14.1
1982	1,142.0	4,913	117.4	15.7
1983	1,377.2	5,870	128.8	15.9
1984	1,572.3	6,640	153.8	18.1
1985	1,823.1	7,598	178.9	18.9
1986	2,125.3	8,774	190.2	19.2
1987	2,350.3	9,615	195.4	19.5
1988	2,602.3	10,534	214.1	20.1
1989	2,857.4	11,545	240.9	21.0
1990	3,223.3	13,000	264.8	21.1
1991	3665.3	14,436	285.4	21.5
1992	4,064.6	15,846	292.3	21.1

Note: Fiscal year ends September 30.

Interest-bearing Public Debt Securities by Kind of Obligation for 1993

	millions of dollars
Total Interest Bearing Public Debt Securities	4,408,567
Marketable Securities	2,904,910
Treasury Bills	658,381
Treasury Notes	1,734,161
Treasury Bonds	497,367
Nonmarketable Securities	1,503,657
U.S. Savings Bonds	167,024
Foreign Government and Public Securities	42,459
Government Account	1,114,289
Other	179,886

Maturity Distribution of Securities Held by Private Investors for 1993

	millions of dollars
Amount Outstanding Privately Held	2,562,336
Maturity Class	
Within 1 year	858,135
1 to 5 years	978,714
5 to 10 years	306,663
10 to 20 years	94,346
Over 20 years	324,479
Average Length	
Years	5
Month	10

Estimated Ownership of Public Debt by Private Investors
September 1993

	billions of dollars
Total	2,938.0
Commercial Banks	306.0
Non Bank Investors	2,677.0
Individuals	305.8
Savings Bonds	169.1
Other Securities	136.7
Insurance Companies	210.0
Money Market Funds	75.2
Corporations	215.6
State & Local Government	558.0
Foreign	592.3
Other	720.0

Percentage of U.S. Debt Owned by Americans

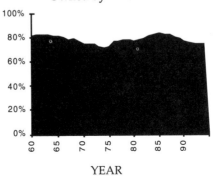

YEAR

Financial Review

45

TAXES

1993 Individual Tax Rates

There are four tax rates for 1993: 15%, 28%, 31% and 36%. The dollar bracket amounts are adjusted each year for inflation.

Tax Rate	Taxable Income
Single	
15%	$0-22,100
28%	$22,101-53,500
31%	$53,100-115,000
36%	$115,001-250,000
Married Filing Jointly or Widow(er)	
15%	$0-36,900
28%	$36,901-89,150
31%	$89,151-140,000
36%	$140,001-250,000
Married Filing Separately	
15%	$0-18,450
28%	$18,451-44,575
31%	$44,576-70,000
36%	$70,001-125,000

Tax Rate	Taxable Income
Head of Household	
15%	$0-29,600
28%	$29,601-76,400
31%	$76,401-127,500
36%	$127,501-250,000

There is also a 10% surtax on taxable incomes over $250,000. This provision creates a marginal top tax rate of 39.6%. The maximum tax rate on net capital gains for an individual, estate or trust is 28%.

1993 Corporate Income Tax Rates

Taxable Income	Tax Rate
$0-50,000	15%
$50,001-75,000	25%
$75,001-10 million	34%
over $10 million	35%

Above $15 million there is an additonal 5% tax and above $18.3 million corporations pay a flat rate of 35%. In addtion, personal service corporations such as attorneys or doctors also pay a flat rate of 35%.

COST OF COLLECTING FEDERAL TAXES AND COLLECTIONS BY PRINCIPAL SOURCES

	1992	1991	1990	1989	1988	1970
U. S. population (in thousands)	256,167	252,901	251,329	249,412	246,329	204,878
Number of IRS employees	116,673	115,628	111,858	114,758	114,873	68,683
Cost to govt. of collecting $100 in taxes	$0.58	$0.56	$0.52	$0.51	$0.54	$0.45
Tax per capita	$4,375.27	$4,343.84	$4,203.12	$4,062.84	$3,792.15	$955.31
Collections by principal sources (in thousands of dollars)	$1,120,799,558	$1,086,851,401	$1,056,365,652	$1,013,322,133	$935,106,594	$195,722,096
Income and profits taxes						
Individual	557,723,156	546,876,876	540,228,408	515,731,504	473,666,566	103,651,585
Corporation	117,950,796	113,598,569	110,016,539	117,014,564	109,682,554	35,036,983
Employment taxes	400,080,904	384,451,220	367,219,321	345,625,586	318,038,990	37,449,188
Estate and gift taxes	11,479,116	11,473,141	11,761,939	8,973,146	7,784,445	3,680,076
Alcohol taxes	NOTE 4	NOTE 4	NOTE 4	NOTE 4	NOTE 4	4,746,382
Tobacco taxes	NOTE 4	NOTE 4	NOTE 4	NOTE 4	NOTE 4	2,094,212
Manufacturers' excise taxes	NOTE 3	NOTE 3	NOTE 3	NOTE 3	NOTE 3	6,683,061
All other taxes	33,565,587	30,451,596	27,139,445	25,977,333	25,934,040	2,380,609

NOTE: For fiscal year ending September 30th. NOTE 2: Alcohol and tobacco tax collections are included in the "All other taxes" amount. NOTE 3: Manufacturers' excise taxes are included in the "All other taxes" amount. NOTE 4: Alcohol and tobacco tax collections are now collected and reported by the Bureau of Alcohol, Tobacco, and Firearms. *Source:* IRS 1992 Annual Report.

Federal Income Tax Comparisons:

Taxes at Selected Rate Brackets after Standard Deductions and Personal Exemptions [1]:

Adjusted Gross Income	Single return listing no dependents				Joint return listing two dependents			
	1993	1992	1991	1975	1993	1992	1991	1975
$10,000	$593	$615	$668	$1,506	$-1,511	$-1,384[2]	$1,235[2]	$829
$20,000	2,093	2,115	2,168	4,153	236	408	702	2,860
$30,000	3,833	3,960	4,201	8,018	2,160	2,220	2,355	5,804
$40,000	6,633	6,760	7,001	12,765	3,660	3,720	3,855	9,668
$50,000	9,433	9,560	9,801	18,360	5,160	5,220	5,576	14,260

NOTE (1) For comparison purposes, tax rate schedules were used. NOTE (2) Refund was based on a basic earned income credit for families with dependent children.

Who Must File a Return

You must file a return if you are:	and your gross income is at least:
• Single (legally separated, divorced, or married living apart from spouse with dependent child) and are under 65	$6,050
• Single (legally separated, divorced or married living apart from spouse with dependent child) and are 65 or older	$6,950
• Head of household under age 65	$7,800
• Head of household over age 65	$8,700
• Married, filing jointly, living together at end of year (or at date of death of spouse), and both are under 65	$10,900
• Married, filing jointly, living together at end of year (or at date of death of spouse), and one is 65 or older	$11,600
• Married, filing jointly, living together at end of year (or at date of death of spouse), and both are 65 or older	$12,300
• Married, filing separate return, or married but not living together at end of year	$2,350

Source: World Almanac 1994

Tax Highlights
Omnibus Budget Reconciliation Act 1993

Individual Income Taxes. The act increase the top tax rate to 36% for joint filers with taxable income over $140,000, heads of households with taxable income over $127,500, and singles with taxable income of more than %115,000. Congress also added a 10% surcharge on taxable income of more than $250,000. This provision creates a marginal top tax rate of 39.6% and is retroactive to January 1, 1993.

Social Security Benefits. Effective January 1, 1994, retirees whose incomes, including half their Social Security benefits, exceed $34,000 for singles or $44,00 for married couples filing jointly will pay income tax on up to 85% of their benefits.

Estate and Gift Taxes. The act reinstates the 1992 tp tax rate of 52% on estates between $2.5 million and $3 million, and 55% on estates of more than $3 million. On taxable estates above $10 million an additional tax of 5% of the transfer above $10 million.

Corporate Tax Rates. The act increases the top tax rate for corporations with taxable income over $10 million per year from 34% to 35%. The tax rate for qualified personal service corporations also increases from 34% to 35%.

Moving Expense Deduction. For expenses incurred after 1993, moving expense deductions associated with a new job will be limited. Deductions for meals while traveling, living expenses in temporary quarters, and the cost of selling an old residence or buying or renting a new residence will no longer be deductible.

Business Meals and Entertainment. The act reduces the proportion of qualified business meals and entertainment costs that can be deducted as business expenses up to 50% starting in 1994. Congress eliminated the deduction as a business expense of dues in business, social, athletic, luncheon, sporting, and country clubs, including airport and hotel clubs.

Lobbying Expenses. the act eliminates the business deduction for lobbying Congress and federal, state, and local government agencies, beginning in 1994.

Energy Tax. The act imposes a 4.3 cents-per-gallon tax on transportation fuels. Commercial airline fuel is exempt till 1995.

Medicare Tax. In 1994, the $135,000 limit on earned income subject to the payroll tax for Medicare has been repealed. Therefore all wages will be subject to the Medicare tax of 1.45% for both employers and employees. Self-employed individuals will pay a 2.9% Medicare tax on their net self-employed income.

Earned Income Tax Credit. The tax credit rate increases for low-income working taxpayers starting in 1994. A credit of up to $300 is created for childless low income worker over 25 years of age and below 65 years. The Young Child Care Credit and Supplemental Health Insurance Credit are repealed.

Rental Passive Losses. The act allows certain real estate professionals to use losses from rental real estate to offset other nonpassive income, such as wages and self-employment profits.

Charitable Contributions. Taxpayers deducting charitable contributions of $250 or more will have to obtain written substantiation from the charity before filing.

Equipment Write-off. Congress elected to allow small businesses to deduct as an expense up to $17,5000 of the cost of new equipment.

Retirement Plans. The new law reduced from $235,840 to $150,000 the level of compensation for which tax-deferred contributions can be made to retirement plans.

Alternative Minimum Tax. Retroactive to January 1, 1993, the 24% AMT rate has been replaced with a two-tiered tax rate of 26% and 28%.

Estates and Trusts. Retroactive to January 1, 1993, the tax rates for the taxable incomes of estates and trust has increased similarly to the individual income tax rate.

Financial Review

National Leadership in the Capital

Editor's Note: These listings are subject to change since the original gathering of this group of personnel.

President — William Jefferson Clinton
Vice President — Albert Gore, Jr.

Terms of office of the president and vice president:
January 20, 1993, to January 20, 1997.

No person may be elected president of the United States for more than two, 4-year terms.

The Cabinet

Secretary of State — Warren M. Christopher
Secretary of Treasury — Robert Rubin
Secretary of Defense — William Perry
Attorney General — Janet Reno
Secretary of Interior — Dan Glickman
Secretary of Agriculture — Mike Espy
Secretary of Commerce — Ronald H. Brown
Secretary of Labor — Robert B. Reich
Sec. of Health and Human Services — Donna E. Shalala
Sec. of Housing & Urban Development — Henry G. Cisneros
Secretary of Transportation — Federico F. Pena
Secretary of Energy — Hazel R. O'Leary
Secretary of Education — Richard W. Riley
Secretary of Veterans Affairs — Jesse Brown

The White House Staff

(You can write to: 1600 Pennsylvania Avenue, NW, Washington, D.C. 20500 White House Info: 202/456-1414)

Chief of Staff — Leon E. Panetta
Assts. to the President & Deputy Chiefs of Staff — Harold Ickes and Phil Lader
Counselor to the President — Bruce Lindsey
Senior Advisor to the President — George Stephanopoulos
Counselor to the President — David Gergen
Assistant to the President:
  Counsel to the President on Domestic Policy — Carol Rasco
  Public Events & Initiatives — Marcia Hale
  Science & Technology — Dr. John H. Gibbons
  Press Secretary — Dee Dee Myers
  Legislative Affairs — Howard Paster
  Communications — Mark Gearan
  Economic & Domestic Affairs — Robert Rubin
  Management & Admin. — David Watkins
  Cabinet Secretary — Christine A. Varney
  National Security — W. Anthony Lake
  Staff Secretary — John Podesta
  National Service — Eli Segal
  Media Affairs — Jeff Eller
AIDS Policy Coordinator — Kristine M. Gebbie

Executive Agencies

Council of Economic Advisers — Laura D'Andrea Tyson, chmn.
National Economic Council — Robert Rubin, dir.
Central Intelligence Agency — R. James Woolsey, dir.
Office of Nat'l. Drug Control Policy — Lee P. Brown, dir.
Office of Management and Budget — Alice Rivlin, dir.
U.S. Trade Representative — Michael Kantor
Council on Environmental Quality — Ray Clark, chmn.

Department of State

(You can write to: 2201 C Street, NW Washington, D.C. 20520)

Secretary of State — Warren M. Christopher
Deputy Secretary — Clifton R. Wharton, Jr.
Under Secretary for Political Affairs — Peter Tarnoff
Under Secretary for International Security Affairs — Lynn Davis
Under Sec. for Mgmt. — Richard Moose
Under Secretary for Global Affairs — Timothy Wirth
Legal Advisor — Sherman M. Funk
Assistant Secretaries for:
  Administration — Patrick F. Kennedy
  African Affairs — George E. Moose
  Consular Affairs — Mary A. Ryan
  Diplomatic Security — Tony Quainton
  East Asian & Pacific Affairs — Winston Lord
  European & Business Affairs — Daniel Tarullo
  Human Rights/Humanitarian Affairs — John H. F. Shattuck
  Intelligence & Research — Tobi Gati
  Inter-American Affairs — Alexander Watson
  International Organization Affairs — Douglas J. Bennett, Jr.
  Legislative Affairs — Wendy R. Sherman
  Near-Eastern & South Asian Affairs — Edward Djerejian
  Oceans, International Environmental & Scientific Affairs — Elinor G. Constable
  Politico-Military Affairs — Robert L. Galucci
  Public Affairs — Thomas Dinilon
  South Asian Affairs — Robin Raphel

Department of the Treasury

(You can write to: 1500 Pennsylvania Avenue, NW Washington, D.C. 20220)

Secretary of the Treasury — Lloyd Bentsen
Deputy Secretary of the Treasury — Roger Altman
Under Secretary for Domestic Finance — Frank N. Newman
Under Secretary for Int'l. Affairs — Lawrence Summers
General Counsel — Jean Hanson
Assistant Secretaries for:
  Economic Policy — Alicia Hancock Munnell
  Enforcement — Ronald K. Noble

International Affairs — Jeffrey Shafer
Legislative Affairs — Mary B. Levy
Public Affairs & Public Liaison —
Jack R. DeVore
Tax Policy — Leslie B. Samuels
Bureaus:
Comptroller of the Currency —
Eugene A. Ludwig
Customs — George J. Weise, comm.
Engraving and Printing —
Peter H. Daley, dir.
**Federal Law Enforcement Training
Center** — Charles F. Rinkevich, dir.
Internal Revenue Service —
Margaret Richardson, comm.
Mint — David Ryder, dir.
Public Debt — Richard L. Gregg, comm.
U.S. Secret Service — Guy Caputo, act.

Department of Defense (You can write to:
The Pentagon
Washington, D.C. 20301)

Secretary of Defense — William Perry
Under Sec. for Acquisitions — John Deutch
Under Secretary for Policy — Frank Wisner
Asst. Secretaries for:
Policy & Plans — Graham T. Allison
Public Affairs — Kathleen DeLaski
Reserve Affairs — Deborah Lee
Special Operations & Low Intensity
Comptroller — John Hamre
General Counsel — Jamie Gorelick
Administration — Ann Reese, dir.
Chairman, Joint Chiefs of Staff —
Gen. John Shalikashvili
Secretary of the Army — Togo West
Secretary of the Navy — John Dalton
Secretary of the Air Force — Sheila Widnall

Department of Justice (You can write to:
Constitution Avenue & 10th Street, NW
Washington, D.C. 20530)

Attorney General — Janet Reno
Dep. Attorney General — Philip B. Heymann
Assoc. Attorney General — Webster L.
Hubbell
Solicitor General — Drew Days, III
Assistants:
Antitrust Division — Anne Bingaman
Civil Division — Frank Hunger
Civil Rights Division — James Turner, act.
**Environment & Natural Resources
Division** — Gerald Torres
Legal Counsel — Walter Delinger
Legal Policy — Eleanor Acheson
Legislative Affairs — Sheila Foster
Federal Bureau of Investigation —
Louis J. Freeh, dir.
Executive Office for Immigration Review —
Bureau of Prisons — Kathleen M. Hawk, dir.
Comm. Relations Service — Jeffrey Weiss,
act. dir.

Drug Enforcement Adm. — Robert C. Bonner
Office of Special Counsel for Immigration
Executive Office for U.S. Trustees —
John Logan, dir.
Executive Office for U.S. Attorneys —
Anthony C. Moscato, dir.
Immigration & Naturalization Service —
Gene McNary
Pardon Attorney — Margaret Love
U. S. Parole Commission — Edward F.
Reilly, Jr., chmn.
U.S. Marshals Service — Eduardo Gonzalez, dir.
U.S. National Central Bureau of Interpol —
Shelley G. Altenstadtero, chief.

Department of the Interior (You can write to:
C Street between 18th & 19th Streets, NW
Washington, D.C. 20240)

Secretary of the Interior — Bruce Babbitt
Deputy Secretary — Robert Hattoy, act.
Asst. Secretaries for:
Fish, Wildlife, and Parks — George T.
Framton, Jr.
Indian Affairs — Ada Deer
Land & Minerals — Robert Armstrong
Policy, Budget & Management — Bonnie
R. Cohen
Ter. & Int'l. Affairs — Leslie Turner
Water & Science — Elizabeth A. Reike
Bureau of Land Management — Jim Baca, dir.
Bureau of Mines — Herman Enzer, act. dir.
Bureau of Reclamation — Daniel T.
Beard, comm.
Fish & Wildlife Service — Mollie Beattie, dir.
Geological Survey — Robert Hirsch, act. dir.
National Park Service — Roger Kennedy, dir.
Public Affairs — Kevin Sweeney, dir.
**Office of Congressional and Legislative
Affairs** — Stephanie Solien
Solicitor — John D. Leshy

Department of Agriculture
(You can write to:
The Mall, 12th & 14th Streets
Washington, D.C. 20250)

Secretary of Agriculture — Mike Espy
Asst. Secretaries for:
Administration — Wardell Townsend, Jr.
Congressional Relations — Robin Rorapaugh
Economics — Keith Collins, act.
Food & Consumer Services — Ellen Haas
Int'l. Affairs & Commod. Programs —
Eugene Moos
Marketing and Inspection Services —
Eugene Branstool
Natural Resources & Environment —
James Lyons
Science & Education — R. D. Plowman, act.
General Counsel — James Gilliland
Inspector General — Charles Gillum, act.
Public Affairs — Ali Webb
Press Secretary — Steve Kinsella

Department of Commerce

(You can write to: 14th Street between Constitution & E. Street, NW Washington, D. C. 20230)

Secretary of Commerce — Ronald H. Brown
Chief of Staff — Carole Timble
Asst. Secretaries for:
   Export Enforcement — Douglas Lavin
   Import Administration — Loretta Dunn
   Oceans & Atmosphere — Douglas K. Hall
Under Secy. for International Trade — Jeffrey Garten
Under Secy. for Econ. Affairs — Everett Ehrlich
Under Secy. for Technology — Mary Lowe Good
Nat'l. Inst. for Standards & Techn. — Arati Prabhakar, dir.
Minority Business Development Agency — Joe Lira
Public Affairs — Eric Ruff, dir.

Department of Labor

(You can write to: 200 Constitution Avenue, NW Washington, D. C. 20210)

Secretary of Labor — Robert B. Reich
Deputy Secretary — Thomas P. Glynn
Chief of Staff — Kathryn Higgins
Asst. Secretaries for:
   Congress. & Intergovernmental Affairs — Geri Palast
   Employment & Training — Doug Ross
   Occupational Safety & Health — Joseph Dear
   Pension & Welfare Benefits — Olena Berg
   Policy — John Donahue
   Public Affairs — Anne Lewis
Solicitor of Labor — Thomas S. Williamson
Women's Bureau — Karen Nussbaum, dir.
Inspector General — vacant
Bureau of Labor Statistics — Katharine Abraham

Department of Health and Human Services

(You can write to: 200 Independence Avenue, SW Washington, D. C. 20201)

Secretary of HHS — Donna E. Shalala
Asst. Secretaries for:
   Children & Families — Mary Jo Bane
   Health — James Mason, M.D.
   Legislation — Jerry D. Klepner
   Management & Budget — Kenneth Apfel
   Personnel Admin. — Thomas McFee
   Planning & Evaluation — David T. Ellwood
   Public Affairs — Avis LaVelle
General Counsel — Harriet Rabb
Inspector General — June Gibbs Brown
Surgeon General — Jocelyn Elders
Social Security Adm. — Shirley Sears Chater

Department of Housing & Urban Development

(You can write to: 451 7th Street, SW Washington, D. C. 20410)

Secretary of Housing & Urban Development —
   Henry G. Cisneros
Deputy Secretary — Terrence Duvernay
Asst. Secretaries for:

   Community Planning & Development —
    Andrew Cuomo
   Fair Housing & Equal Opportunity —
    Robert A. Achtenberg
   Field Management — Frank Wing
   Housing & Federal Housing Commissioner —
    Nicolas P. Retsinas
   Labor Relations — Joseph A. Scudero
   Congressional & Intergovernmental Relations —
    William J. Gilmartin
   Policy Dvlpt. & Research — Michael Stegman
   Public Affairs — Jean Nolan
   Public & Indian Housing — Joseph Shuldiner
General Counsel — Nelson Diaz
Inspector General — Susan Gaffney

Department of Transportation

(You can write to: 400 7th Street, SW Washington, D. C. 20590)

Secretary of Transportation — Federico F. Pena
Deputy Secretary — Mortimer L. Downey
Asst. Secretaries for:
   Administration — Jon H. Seymour
   Budget & Programs — Louise Stroll
   Public Affairs — Richard I. Mintz
U. S. Coast Guard Commandant — Adm. J. W. Kime
Federal Aviation Admin. — David Hinson
Federal Highway Admin — Rodney Slater
Federal Railroad Admin. — Jolene Molitoris
Maritime Admin. — Albert Herberger
Federal Transit — Gordon J. Linton
St. Lawrence Seaway Dvlpt. Corp. — Stan E. Parris

Department of Energy

(You can write to: 1000 Independence Avenue, SW Washington, D. C. 20585)

Secretary of Energy — Hazel R. O'Leary
Deputy Secretary — William H. White
General Counsel — Robert Nordhaus
Inspector General — John C. Layton
Asst. Secretaries for:
   Congressional & Intergovernmental Affairs —
    William Taylor
   Defense Programs — Victor Reis
   Domestic & Int'l. Energy Policy — Susan Tierney
   Environment, Safety & Health — Tara Jeanne O'Toole
Energy Information Adm. — Jay Hakes, adm.
Econ. Regulatory Adm. — Jay Thompson, act. adm.
Fed. Energy Regulatory Comm. — Elizabeth Moler, chair.
Energy Research — Martha Krebs

Department of Education

(You can write to: 400 Maryland Avenue, SW Washington, D. C. 20202)

Secretary of Education — Richard W. Riley
Under Secretary — Marshall S. Smith
Deputy Secretary — Madeline Kumin
Chief of Staff — Polly Gault
Inspector General — James B. Thomas, Jr.
General Counsel — Judith Winston

Asst. Secretaries for:
  Adult & Vocational Education —
    Augusta Kappner
  Civil Rights — Norman V. Cantu
  Educational Research & Improvement —
    Porter Robinson
  Elementary & Secondary Education —
    Thomas W. Payzant
  Legislation & Congressional Affairs —
    Kay Casstevens
Postsecondary Education —
  David Longanecker
Special Education & Rehabilitative Svcs. —
  Judith Heumann

Department of Veterans Affairs
(You can write to:
810 Vermont Avenue, NW
Washington, D.C. 20420)

Secretary of Veterans Affairs — Jesse Brown
Deputy — Hershel W. Gober
Asst. Secretaries for:
  Acquisition & Facilities — Gary Krump, act.
  Congressional Affairs — Edward P. Scott
  Finance & Information Resources Mgmt. —
    D. Mark Catlett
  Human Resources & Adm. —
    Eugene Brickhouse
  Policy & Planning — Victor P. Raymond
  Public & Intergovernmental Affairs —
    Kathy E. Jurado
Inspector General — Stephen Trodden
National Cemetary System —
  Jerry W. Bowen, dir.
General Counsel — Mary Lou Keener
Board of Veterans Appeals —
  Charles L. Cragin, chmn.

Editor's Note:

As a citizen of the United States, you should always feel free to write or call any member of the government, especially those who represent you directly in Congress.

This is why we have provided you with the names and addresses of the administration and all members of the U.S. Congress.

Your representatives and others serving in the government want to hear from you and how you feel about issues that face this nation and your particular area of the country.

One letter or call can make a difference in the way a U.S. Senator or U.S. Representative votes in Washington, D.C.

Your representatives in Washington, D.C., also have offices in their states. You are encouraged to visit your representatives in person with your questions and comments.

Public and school libraries have references explaining how to effectively communicate with our leaders.

The Legislature

ALABAMA

Senators

Senator Howell T. Heflin (D)
728 Hart Senate
Office Building
Washington, D. C. 20510
Phone: 202-224-4124
FAX: 202-224-3149

Senator Richard C. Shelby (D)
509 Hart Senate
Office Building
Washington, D. C. 20510
Phone: 202-224-5744
FAX: 202-224-3416

Representatives

Rep. Sonny Callahan (R)
(First District)
2418 Rayburn House
Office Building
Washington, D. C. 20515
Phone: 202-225-4931
FAX: 202-225-0562

Rep. Terry Everett (R)
(Second District)
208 Cannon House
Office Building
Washington, D. C. 20515
Phone: 202-225-2901
FAX: (Unlisted)

Rep. Glen Browder (D)
(Third District)
1221 Longworth House
Office Building
Washington, D. C. 20515
Phone: 202-225-3261
FAX: 202-225-9020

Rep. Tom Bevill (D)
(Fourth District)
2302 Rayburn House
Office Building
Washington, D. C. 20515
Phone: 202-225-4876
FAX: 202-225-1604

Rep. Robert "Bud" Cramer (D)
(Fifth District)
1318 Longworth House
Office Building
Washington, D. C. 20515
Phone: 202-225-4801
FAX: 202-225-4392

Rep. Spencer Bachus (R)
(Sixth District)
216 Cannon House
Office Building
Washington, D. C. 20515
Phone: 202-225-4921
FAX: 202-225-2082

Rep. Earl F. Hilliard (D)
(Seventh District)
1007 Longworth House
Office Building
Washington, D. C. 20515
Phone: 202-225-2665
FAX: 202-226-0772

ALASKA

Senators

Senator Ted Stevens (R)
522 Hart Senate
Office Building
Washington, D. C. 20510
Phone: 202-224-3004
FAX: 202-224-2354

Senator Frank H. Murkowski (R)
706 Hart Senate
Office Building
Washington, D. C. 20510
Phone: 202-224-6665
FAX: 202-224-5301

Representative At Large

Rep. Don Young (R)
2331 Rayburn House
Office Building
Washington, D. C. 20515
Phone: 202-225-5765
FAX: 202-225-0425

ARIZONA

Senators

Senator John Kyl (R)
328 Hart Senate
Office Building
Washington, D. C. 20510
Phone: 202-224-4521
FAX: 202-224-2302

Senator John S. McCain (R)
111 Russell Senate
Office Building
Washington, D. C. 20510
Phone: 202-224-2235
FAX: 202-228-2862

Representatives

Rep. Matt Salmon (R)
(First District)
1607 Longworth House
Office Building
Washington, D. C. 20515
Phone: 202-225-2635
FAX: 202-225-2607

Rep. Ed. Pastor (D)
(Second District)
408 Cannon House
Office Building
Washington, D. C. 20515
Phone: 202-225-4065
FAX: 202-225-1655

Rep. Bob Stump (R)
(Third District)
211 Cannon House
Office Building
Washington, D. C. 20515
Phone: 202-225-4576
FAX: 202-225-6328

Rep. John Shadegg (R)
(Fourth District)
2440 Rayburn House
Office Building
Washington, D. C. 20515
Phone: 202-225-3361
FAX: 202-225-1143

Rep. James Thomas Kolbe (R)
(Fifth District)
405 Cannon House
Office Building
Washington, D. C. 20515
Phone: 202-225-2542
FAX: 202-225-0378

Rep. J. D. Hayworth (R)
(Sixth District)
1024 Longworth House
Office Building
Washington, D. C. 20515
Phone: 202-225-2190
FAX: 202-225-8819

ARKANSAS

Senators

Senator Dale Bumpers (D)
229 Dirksen Senate
Office Building
Washington, D. C. 20510
Phone: 202-224-4843
FAX: 202-224-6435

Senator David H. Pryor (D)
267 Russell Senate
Office Building
Washington, D. C. 20510
Phone: 202-224-2353
FAX: 202-224-8261

Representatives

Rep. Blanche Lambert (D)
(First District)
1204 Longworth House
Office Building
Washington, D. C. 20515
Phone: 202-225-4076
FAX: 202-225-4654

Rep. Ray Thornton (D)
(Second District)
1214 Longworth House
Office Building
Washington, D. C. 20515
Phone: 202-225-2506
FAX: 202-225-9273

Rep. Tim Hutchinson (R)
(Third District)
1541 Longworth House
Office Building
Washington, D. C. 20515
Phone: 202-225-4301
FAX: 202-225-7492

Rep. Jay Dickey (R)
(Fourth District)
1338 Longworth House
Office Building
Washington, D. C. 20515
Phone: 202-225-3772
FAX: 202-225-1314

Senators

Senator Barbara Boxer (D)
112 Hart Senate
Office Building
Washington, D. C. 20510
Phone: 202-224-3553
FAX: 202-224-6252

Senator Dianne Feinstein (D)
331 Hart Senate
Office Building
Washington, D. C. 20510
Phone: 202-224-3841
FAX: 202-224-0656

Representatives

Rep. Frank Riggs (D)
(First District)
114 Cannon House
Office Building
Washington, D. C. 20515
Phone: 202-225-3311
FAX: 202-225-7710

Rep. Wally Herger (R)
(Second District)
2433 Longworth House
Office Building
Washington, D. C. 20515
Phone: 202-225-3076
FAX: 202-225-1609

Rep. Vic Fazio (D)
(Third District)
2113 Rayburn House
Office Building
Washington, D. C. 20515
Phone: 202-225-5716
FAX: 202-225-0354

Rep. John T. Doolittle (R)
(Fourth District)
1542 Longworth House
Office Building
Washington, D. C. 20515
Phone: 202-225-2511
FAX: 202-225-5444

Rep. Robert T. Matsui (D)
(Fifth District)
2311 Rayburn House
Office Building
Washington, D. C. 20515
Phone: 202-225-7163
FAX: 202-225-0566

Rep. Lynn Woolsey (D)
(Sixth District)
439 Cannon House
Office Building
Washington, D. C. 20515
Phone: 202-225-5161
FAX: 202-225-5163

Rep. George Miller (D)
(Seventh District)
2205 Rayburn House
Office Building
Washington, D. C. 20515
Phone: 202-225-2095
FAX: 202-225-5609

Rep. Nancy Pelosi (D)
(Eighth District)
240 Cannon House Office Building
Washington, D. C. 20515
Phone: 202-225-4965
FAX: 202-225-8259

Rep. Ronald V. Dellums (D)
(Ninth District)
2108 Rayburn House
Office Building
Washington, D. C. 20515
Phone: 202-225-2661
FAX: 202-225-9817

Rep. Bill Baker (R)
(Tenth District)
1714 Longworth House
Office Building
Washington, D. C. 20515
Phone: 202-225-1880
FAX: 202-225-2150

Rep. Richard W. Pombo (R)
(Eleventh District)
1519 Longworth House
Office Building
Washington, D. C. 20515
Phone: 202-225-1947
FAX: 202-226-0861

Rep. Tom Lantos (D)
(Twelfth District)
2182 Rayburn House
Office Building
Washington, D. C. 20515
Phone: 202-225-3531
FAX: 202-225-3127

Rep. Fortney H. "Pete" Stark
(D) (Thirteenth District)
239 Cannon House Office Building
Washington, D. C. 20515
Phone: 202-225-5065
FAX: (Unlisted)

Rep. Anna G. Eshoo (D)
(Fourteenth District)
1505 Longworth House
Office Building
Washington, D. C. 20515
Phone: 202-225-8104
FAX: 202-225-8890

Rep. Norman Y. Mineta (D)
(Fifteenth District)
2221 Rayburn House
Office Building
Washington, D. C. 20515
Phone: 202-225-2631
FAX: (Unlisted)

Rep. Zoe Lofgren (D)
(Sixteenth District)
2307 Rayburn House Office Building
Washington, D. C. 20515
Phone: 220-225-3072
FAX: 202-225-9460

Rep. Sam Farr (D)
(Seventeenth District)
1216 Longworth House
Office Building
Washington, D. C. 20515
Phone: 202-225-2861
FAX: 202-225-2861

Rep. Gary Condit (D)
(Eighteenth District)
1123 Longworth House
Office Building
Washington, D. C. 20515
Phone: 202-225-6131
FAX: 202-225-0819

Rep. George Radanovich (R)
(Nineteenth District)
1226 Longworth House
Office Building
Washington, D. C. 20515
Phone: 202-225-4540
FAX: 202-225-5274

Rep. Calvin Dooley (D)
(Twentieth District)
1227 Longworth House
Office Building
Washington, D. C. 20515
Phone: 202-225-3341
FAX: 202-225-9308

Rep. William M. Thomas (R)
(Twenty-First District)
2209 Rayburn House
Office Building
Washington, D. C. 20515
Phone: 202-225-2915
FAX: 202-225-8798

Rep. Michael Huffington (R)
(Twenty-Second District)
113 Cannon House
Office Building
Washington, D. C. 20515
Phone: 202-225-3601
FAX: 202-226-1015

Rep. Elton William Gallegly (R)
(Twenty-Third District)
2441 Rayburn House
Office Building
Washington, D. C. 20515
Phone: 202-225-5811
FAX: 202-225-0713

Rep. Anthony C. Beilenson (D)
(Twenty-Fourth District)
2465 Rayburn House
Office Building
Washington, D. C. 20515
Phone: 202-225-5911
FAX: (Unlisted)

Rep. Howard P. "Buck" McKeon
(R) (Twenty-Fifth District)
307 Cannon House
Office Building
Washington, D. C. 20515
Phone: 202-225-1956
FAX: 202-226-0683

Rep. Howard L. Berman (D)
(Twenty-Sixth District)
2201 Rayburn House
Office Building
Washington, D. C. 20515
Phone: 202-225-4695
FAX: 202-225-5279

Rep. Carlos J. Moorhead (R)
(Twenty-Seventh District)
2346 Rayburn House
Office Building
Washington, D. C. 20515
Phone: 202-225-4176
FAX: 202-226-1279

Rep. David Timothy Dreier (R)
(Twenty-Eighth District)
411 Cannon House
Office Building
Washington, D. C. 20515
Phone: 202-225-2305
FAX: 202-225-4745

Rep. Henry A. Waxman (D)
(Twenty-Ninth District)
2408 Rayburn House
Office Building
Washington, D. C. 20515
Phone: 202-225-3976
FAX: 202-225-4099

Rep. Xavier Becerra (D)
(Thirtieth District)
1710 Longworth House
Office Building
Washington, D. C. 20515
Phone: 202-225-6235
FAX: 202-225-2202

Rep. Matthew G. Martinez (D)
(Thirty-First District)
2231 Rayburn House
Office Building
Washington, D. C. 20515
Phone: 202-225-5464
FAX: 202-225-5467

Rep. Julian Carey Dixon (D)
(Thirty-Second District)
2400 Rayburn House
Office Building
Washington, D. C. 20515
Phone: 202-225-7084
FAX: 202-225-4091

Rep. Lucille Roybal-Allard (D)
(Thirty-Third District)
324 Cannon House
Office Building
Washington, D. C. 20515
Phone: 202-225-1766
FAX: 202-226-0350

Rep. Esteban E. Torres (D)
(Thirty-Fourth District)
1740 Longworth House
Office Building
Washington, D. C. 20515
Phone: 202-225-5256
FAX: 202-225-9711

Rep. Maxine Waters (D)
(Thirty-Fifth District)
1207 Longworth House
Office Building
Washington, D. C. 20515
Phone: 202-225-2201
FAX: 202-225-7854

Rep. Jane Harman (D)
(Thirty-Sixth District)
325 Cannon House
Office Building
Washington, D. C. 20515
Phone: 202-225-8220
FAX: 202-226-0684

Rep. Walter R. Tucker, III (D)
(Thirty-Seventh District)
419 Cannon House
Office Building
Washington, D. C. 20515
Phone: 202-225-7924
FAX: 202-225-7926

Rep. Steve Horn (R)
(Thirty-Eighth District)
1023 Longworth House
Office Building
Washington, D. C. 20515
Phone: 202-225-6676
FAX: 202-226-1012

Rep. Ed Royce (R)
(Thirty-Ninth District)
1404 Longworth House
Office Building
Washington, D. C. 20515
Phone: 202-225-4111
FAX: 202-226-0335

Rep. Jerry Lewis (R)
(Fortieth District)
2312 Rayburn House
Office Building
Washington, D. C. 20515
Phone: 202-225-5861
FAX: 202-225-6498

Rep. Jay C. Kim (R)
(Forty-First District)
502 Cannon House
Office Building.
Washington, D. C. 20515
Phone: 202-225-3201
FAX: 202-226-1485

Rep. George E. Brown, Jr. (D)
(Forty-Second District)
2300 Rayburn House
Office Building.
Washington, D. C. 20515
Phone: 202-225-6161
FAX: 202-225-8671

Rep. Ken Calvert (R)
(Forty-Third District)
1523 Longworth House
Office Building
Washington, D. C. 20515
Phone: 202-225-1986
FAX: (Unavailable at T.O.P.)

Rep. Sonny Bono (R)
(Forty-Fourth District)
2422 Longworth House
Office Building
Washington, D. C. 20515
Phone: 202-225-5330
FAX: 202-226-1040

Rep. Dana Rohrabacher (R)
(Forty-Fifth District)
1027 Longworth House
Office Building
Washington, D. C. 20515
Phone: 202-225-2415
FAX: 202-225-0145

Rep. Robert K. Dornan (R)
(Forty-Sixth District)
2402 Rayburn House
Office Building
Washington, D. C. 20515
Phone: 202-225-2965
FAX: 202-225-3694

Rep. C. Christopher Cox (R)
(Forty-Seventh District)
206 Cannon House
Office Building
Washington, D. C. 20515
Phone: 202-225-5611
FAX: 202-225-9177

Rep. Ronald C. Packard (R)
(Forty-Eighth District)
2162 Rayburn House
Office Building
Washington, D. C. 20515
Phone: 202-225-3906
FAX: 202-225-0134

Rep. Brian Bilbray (R)
(Forty-Ninth District)
315 Cannon House
Office Building
Washington, D. C. 20515
Phone: 202-225-2040
FAX: 202-225-2042

Rep. Bob Filner (D)
(Fiftieth District)
504 Cannon House
Office Building
Washington, D. C. 20515
Phone: 202-225-8045
FAX: 202-225-9073

Rep. Randy "Duke"
Cunningham (R)
(Fifty-First District)
117 Cannon House
Office Building
Washington, D. C. 20515
Phone: 202-225-5452
FAX: 202-225-2558

Rep. Duncan Lee Hunter (R)
(Fifty-Second District)
133 Cannon House
Office Building
Washington, D. C. 20515
Phone: 202-225-5672
FAX: 202-225-0235

COLORADO

Senators
Senator Ben Nighthorse
Campbell (D)
380 Russell Senate
Office Building
Washington, D. C. 20510
Phone: 202-224-5852
FAX: 202-224-3714

Senator Hank Brown (R)
716 Hart Senate
Office Building
Washington, D. C. 20510
Phone: 202-224-5941
FAX: 202-224-6471

Representatives
Rep. Patricia S. Schroeder (D)
(First District)
2208 Rayburn House
Office Building
Washington, D. C. 20515
Phone: 202-225-4431
FAX: 202-225-5842

Rep. David E. Skaggs (D)
(Second District)
1124 Longworth House
Office Building
Washington, D. C. 20515
Phone: 202-225-2161
FAX: 202-225-9127

Rep. Scott McInnis (R)
(Third District)
512 Cannon House
Office Building
Washington, D. C. 20515
Phone: 202-225-4761
FAX: 202-226-0622

Rep. Wayne Allard (R)
(Fourth District)
422 Cannon House
Office Building
Washington, D. C. 20515
Phone: 202-225-4676
FAX: 202-225-8630

Rep. Joel Hefley (R)
(Fifth District)
2442 Rayburn House
Office Building
Washington, D. C. 20515
Phone: 202-225-4422
FAX: 202-225-1942

Rep. Dan L. Schaefer (R)
(Sixth District)
2448 Rayburn House
Office Building
Washington, D. C. 20515
Phone: 202-225-7882
FAX: 202-225-7885

CONNECTICUT
Senators
Senator Christopher J. Dodd (D)
444 Russell Senate
Office Building
Washington, D. C. 20510
Phone: 202-224-2823
FAX: 202-224-5431

Senator Joseph I.
Lieberman (D)
316 Hart Senate
Office Building
Washington, D. C. 20510
Phone: 202-224-4041
FAX: 202-224-9750

Representatives
Rep. Barbara B. Kennelly (D)
(First District)
201 Cannon House
Office Building
Washington, D. C. 20515
Phone: 202-225-2265
FAX: 202-225-1031

Rep. Samuel Gejdenson (D)
(Second District)
2416 Rayburn House
Office Building
Washington, D. C. 20515
Phone: 202-225-2076
FAX: 202-225-4977

Rep. Rosa DeLauro (D)
(Third District)
327 Cannon House
Office Building
Washington, D. C. 20515
Phone: 202-225-3661
FAX: 202-225-4890

Rep. Christopher Shays (R)
(Fourth District)
1034 Longworth House
Office Building
Washington, D. C. 20515
Phone: 202-225-5541
FAX: 202-225-9629

Rep. Gary Franks (R)
(Fifth District)
435 Cannon House
Office Building
Washington, D. C. 20515
Phone: 202-225-3822
FAX: 202-225-5085

Rep. Nancy Lee Johnson (R)
(Sixth District)
343 Cannon House
Office Building
Washington, D. C. 20515
Phone: 202-225-4476
FAX: 202-225-4488

DELAWARE
Senators
Senator William V. Roth, Jr. (R)
104 Hart Senate
Office Building
Washington, D. C. 20510
Phone: 202-224-2441
FAX: 202-224-2805

Senator Joseph R. Biden, Jr. (D)
221 Russell Senate
Office Building
Washington, D. C. 20510
Phone: 202-224-5042
FAX: 202-224-0139

Representative At Large
Rep. Michael N. Castle (R)
1205 Longworth House
Office Building
Washington, D. C. 20515
Phone: 202-225-4165
FAX: 202-225-2291

FLORIDA
Senators
Senator Robert Graham (D)
524 Hart Senate
Office Building
Washington, D. C. 20510
Phone: 202-224-3041
FAX: 202-224-2237

Senator Connie Mack, III (R)
517 Hart Senate
Office Building
Washington, D. C. 20510
Phone: 202-224-5274
FAX: 202-224-9365

Representatives
Rep. Joe Scarborough (D)
(First District)
2435 Rayburn House
Office Building
Washington, D. C. 20515
Phone: 202-225-4136
FAX: 202-225-5785

Rep. Pete Peterson (D)
(Second District)
426 Cannon House
Office Building
Washington, D. C. 20515
Phone: 202-225-5235
FAX: 202-225-1586

Rep. Corrine Brown (D)
(Third District)
1037 Longworth House
Office Building
Washington, D. C. 20515
Phone: 202-225-0123
FAX: 202-225-2256

Rep. Tillie Fowler (R)
(Fourth District)
413 Cannon House
Office Building
Washington, D. C. 20515
Phone: 202-225-2501
FAX: 202-226-9318

Rep. Karen L. Thurman (D)
(Fifth District)
130 Cannon House
Office Building
Washington, D. C. 20515
Phone: 202-225-1002
FAX: 202-226-0329

Rep. Cliff Stearns (R)
(Sixth District)
332 Cannon House
Office Building, #2015
Phone: 202-225-5744
FAX: 202-225-3973

Rep. John L. Mica (R)
(Seventh District)
427 Cannon House
Office Building
Washington, D. C. 20515
Phone: 202-225-4035
FAX: 202-226-0821

Rep. Bill McCollum (R)
(Eighth District)
2266 Rayburn House
Office Building
Washington, D. C. 20515
Phone: 202-225-2176
FAX: 202-225-0999

Rep. Michael Bilirakis
(R) (Ninth District)
2240 Rayburn House
Office Building
Washington, D. C. 20515
Phone: 202-225-5755
FAX: 202-225-4085

Rep. C. W. Bill Young (R)
(Tenth District)
2407 Rayburn House
Office Building
Washington, D. C. 20515
Phone: 202-225-5961
FAX: 202-225-9764

Rep. Sam M. Gibbons (D)

(Eleventh District)

2204 Rayburn House
Office Building
Washington, D. C. 20515

Phone: 202-225-3376

FAX: (Unlisted)

Rep. Charles T. Canady (R)

(Twelfth District)

1107 Longworth House
Office Building
Washington, D. C. 20515

Phone: 202-225-1252

FAX: 202-225-2279

Rep. Dan Miller (R)

(Thirteenth District)

510 Cannon House Office Building
Washington, D. C. 20515

Phone: 202-225-5015

FAX: 202-226-0828

Rep. Porter Goss (R)

(Fourteenth District)

330 Cannon House Office Building
Washington, D. C. 20515

Phone: 202-225-2536

FAX: 202-225-6820

Rep. Dave Weldon (D)

(Fifteenth District)

432 Cannon House Office Building
Washington, D. C. 20515

Phone: 202-225-3671

FAX: 202-225-9039

Rep. Mark Foley (R)

(Sixteenth District)

2351 Rayburn House
Office Building
Washington, D. C. 20515

Phone: 202-225-5792

FAX: 202-225-1860

Rep. Carrie Meek (D)

(Seventeenth District)

404 Cannon House
Office Building
Washington, D. C. 20515

Phone: 202-225-4506

FAX: 202-226-0777

Rep. Ileana Ros-Lehtinen (R)

(Eighteenth District)

127 Cannon House
Office Building
Washington, D. C. 20515

Phone: 202-225-3931

FAX: 202-225-5620

Rep. Harry A. Johnston, II (D)

(Nineteenth District)

204 Cannon House Office Building
Washington, D. C. 20515

Phone: 202-225-3001

FAX: 202-225-8791

Rep. Peter Deustch (D)

(Twentieth District)

425 Cannon House Office Building
Washington, D. C. 20515

Phone: 202-225-7931

FAX: 202-225-8456

Rep. Lincoln Diaz-Balart (R)

(Twenty-First District)

509 Cannon House Office Building
Washington, D. C. 20515

Phone: 202-225-4211

FAX: 202-225-8576

Rep. E. Clay Shaw, Jr. (R)

(Twenty-Second District)

2267 Rayburn House
Office Building
Washington, D. C. 20515

Phone: 202-225-3026

FAX: 202-225-8398

Rep. Alcee L. Hastings (D)

(Twenty-Third District)

1039 Longworth House
Office Building
Washington, D. C. 20515

Phone: 202-225-1313

FAX: 202-226-0690

GEORGIA

Senators

Senator Samuel A. Nunn (D)

303 Dirksen Senate Office Building
Washington, D. C. 20510

Phone: 202-224-3521

FAX: 202-224-0072

Senator Paul Coverdell (R)

200 Russell Senate Office Building
Washington, D. C. 20510

Phone: 202-224-3643

FAX: 202-224-8227

Representatives

Rep. Jack Kingston (R)

(First District)

1229 Longworth House
Office Building
Washington, D. C. 20515

Phone: 202-225-5831

FAX: 202-226-2269

Rep. Sanford Bishop (D)

(Second District)

1632 Longworth House
Office Building
Washington, D. C. 20515

Phone: 202-225-3631

FAX: 202-225-2203

Rep. Mac Collins (R)

(Third District)

1118 Longworth House
Office Building
Washington, D. C. 20515

Phone: 202-225-5901

FAX: 202-225-2515

Rep. John Linder (R)

(Fourth District)

1605 Longworth House
Office Building
Washington, D. C. 20515

Phone: 202-225-4272

FAX: 202-225-4696

Rep. John R. Lewis (D)

(Fifth District)

329 Cannon House
Office Building
Washington, D. C. 20515

Phone: 202-225-3801

FAX: 202-225-0351

Rep. Newton L. Gingrich (R)

(Sixth District)

2428 Rayburn House
Office Building
Washington, D. C. 20515

Phone: 202-225-4501

FAX: 202-225-4656

Rep. Robert Barr (D)

(Seventh District)

2303 Rayburn House
Office Building
Washington, D. C. 20515

Phone: 202-225-2931

FAX: 202-225-0473

Rep. Saxby Chambuss (R)

(Eighth District)

2134 Rayburn House
Office Building
Washington, D. C. 20515

Phone: 202-225-6531

FAX: 202-225-7719

Rep. Nathan Deal (D)

(Ninth District)

1406 Longworth House
Office Building
Washington, D. C. 20515

Phone: 202-225-5211

FAX: 202-225-8272

Rep. Charles Norwood (R)

(Tenth District)

226 Cannon House
Office Building
Washington, D. C. 20515

Phone: 202-225-4101

FAX: 202-226-1466

Rep. Cynthia McKinney (D)

(Eleventh District)

124 Cannon House
Office Building
Washington, D. C. 20515

Phone: 202-225-1605

FAX: 202-226-0691

HAWAII

Senators

Senator Daniel K. Inouye (D)

722 Hart Senate
Office Building
Washington, D. C. 20510

Phone: 202-224-3934

FAX: 202-224-6747

Senator Daniel K. Akaka (D)

720 Hart Senate
Office Building
Washington, D. C. 20510

Phone: 202-224-6361

FAX 202-224-2126:

Representatives

Rep. Neil Abercrombie (D)

(First District)

1440 Longworth House
Office Building
Washington, D. C. 20515

Phone: 202-225-2726

FAX: 202-225-4580

Rep. Patsy T. Mink (D)

(Second District)

2135 Rayburn House
Office Building
Washington, D. C. 20515

Phone: 202-225-4906

FAX: 202-225-4987

IDAHO

Senators

Senator Dirk Kempthorne (R)
367 Dirksen Senate
Office Building
Washington, D. C. 20510
Phone: 202-224-6142
FAX: 202-224-5893

Senator Larry Craig (R)
313 Hart Senate
Office Building
Washington, D. C. 20510
Phone: 202-224-2752
FAX: 202-224-2573

Representatives

Rep. Helen Chenoweth (R)
(First District)
1117 Longworth House
Office Building
Washington, D. C. 20515
Phone: 202-225-55
FAX: 202-226-1213

Rep. Michael D. Crapo (R)
(Second District)
437 Cannon House Office Building
Washington, D. C. 20515
Phone: 202-225-5531
FAX: 202-334-1953

ILLINOIS

Senators

Senator Carol Moseley-Braun (D)
320 Hart Senate Office Building
Washington, D. C. 20510
Phone: 202-224-2854
FAX: unlisted

Senator Paul Simon (D)
462 Dirksen Senate
Office Building
Washington, D. C. 20510
Phone: 202-224-2152
FAX: 202-224-0868

Representatives

Rep. Bobby L. Rush (D)
(First District)
1725 Longworth House
Office Building
Washington, D. C. 20515
Phone: 202-225-4372
FAX: 202-226-0333

Rep. Melvin J. Reynolds (D)
(Second District)
514 Cannon House Office Building
Washington, D. C. 20515
Phone: 202-225-0773
FAX: 202-225-0774

Rep. William O. Lipinski (D) (Third District)
1501 Longworth House
Office Building
Washington, D. C. 20515
Phone: 202-225-5701
FAX: 202-225-1012

Rep. Luis V. Gutierrez (D)
(Fourth District)
1208 Longworth House
Office Building
Washington, D. C. 20515
Phone: 202-225-8203
FAX: 202-225-7810

Rep. Michael Flanaghan (D)
(Fifth District)
2111 Rayburn House
Office Building
Washington, D. C. 20515
Phone: 202-225-4061
FAX: 202-225-4064

Rep. Henry John Hyde (R)
(Sixth District)
2110 Rayburn House
Office Building
Washington, D. C. 20515
Phone: 202-225-4561
FAX: 202-226-1240

Rep. Cardiss Collins (D)
(Seventh District)
2308 Rayburn House
Office Building
Washington, D. C. 20515
Phone: 202-225-5006
FAX: 202-225-8396

Rep. Philip Miller Crane (R)
(Eighth District)
233 Cannon House
Office Building
Washington, D. C. 20515
Phone: 202-225-3711
FAX: 202-225-7830

Rep. Sidney R. Yates (D)
(Ninth District)
2109 Rayburn House
Office Building
Washington, D. C. 20515
Phone: 202-225-2111
FAX: 202-225-3493

Rep. John E. Porter (R)
(Tenth District)
1026 Longworth House
Office Building, #2015
Phone: 202-225-4835
FAX: 202-225-0157

Rep. Gerald Weller (R)
(Eleventh District)
1032 Longworth House
Office Building
Washington, D. C. 20515
Phone: 202-225-3635
FAX: 202-225-4447

Rep. Jerry F. Costello (D)
(Twelfth District)
119 Cannon House Office Building
Washington, D. C. 20515
Phone: 202-225-5661
FAX: 202-225-0285

Rep. Harris W. Fawell (R)
(Thirteenth District)
2342 Rayburn House
Office Building
Washington, D. C. 20515
Phone: 202-225-3515
FAX: 202-225-9420

Rep. John D. Hastert (R)
(Fourteenth District)
2453 Rayburn House
Office Building
Washington, D. C. 20515
Phone: 202-225-2976
FAX: 202-225-0697

Rep. Thomas Ewing (R)
(Fifteenth District)
1317 Longworth House
Office Building
Washington, D. C. 20515
Phone: 202-225-2371
FAX: 202-225-8071

Rep. Donald Manzullo (R)
(Sixteenth District)
506 Cannon House Office Building
Washington, D. C. 20515
Phone: 202-225-5676
FAX: 202-225-5284

Rep. Lane Evans (D)
(Seventeenth District)
2335 Rayburn House
Office Building
Washington, D. C. 20515
Phone: 202-225-5905
FAX: 202-225-5396

Rep. Ray LaHood (R)
(Eighteenth District)
2112 Rayburn House
Office Building
Washington, D. C. 20515
Phone: 202-225-6201
FAX: 202-225-9249

Rep. Glenn Poshard (D)
(Nineteenth District)
107 Cannon House
Office Building
Washington, D. C. 20515
Phone: 202-225-5201
FAX: 202-225-1541

Rep. Richard J. Durbin (D)
(Twentieth District)
2463 Rayburn House
Office Building
Washington, D. C. 20515
Phone: 202-225-5271
FAX: 202-225-0170

INDIANA

Senators

Senator Richard Green Lugar (R)
306 Hart Senate Office Building
Washington, D. C. 20510
Phone: 202-224-4814
FAX: 202-224-7877

Senator Daniel R. Coats (R)
404 Russell Senate
Office Building
Washington, D. C. 20510
Phone: 202-224-5623
FAX: 202-224-1966

Representatives

Rep. Peter J. Visclosky (D)
(First District)
2464 Rayburn House
Office Building
Washington, D. C. 20515
Phone: 202-225-2461
FAX: 202-225-2493

Rep. David McIntosh (R)
(Second District)
2217 Rayburn House
Office Building
Washington, D. C. 20515
Phone: 202-225-3021
FAX: 202-225-8140

Rep. Tim Roemer (D)
(Third District)
415 Cannon House Office Building
Washington, D. C. 20515
Phone: 202-225-3915
FAX: 202-225-6798

Rep. Mark Souder (R)
(Fourth District)
1513 Longworth House
Office Building
Washington, D. C. 20515
Phone: 202-225-4436
FAX: 202-225-8810

Rep. Steve Buyer (R)
(Fifth District)
1419 Longworth House
Office Building
Washington, D. C. 20515
Phone: 202-225-5037
FAX: (Unlisted)

Rep. Dan Burton (R)
(Sixth District)
2411 Rayburn House
Office Building
Washington, D. C. 20515
Phone: 202-225-2276
FAX: 202-225-0016

Rep. John T. Myers (R)
(Seventh District)
2372 Rayburn House
Office Building
Washington, D. C. 20515
Phone: 202-225-5805
FAX: 202-225-1649

Rep. John Hostettler (R)
(Eighth District)
306 Cannon House Office Building
Washington, D. C. 20515
Phone: 202-225-4636
FAX: 202-225-4688

Rep. Lee H. Hamilton (D)
(Ninth District)
2187 Rayburn House Office Building
Washington, D. C. 20515
Phone: 202-225-5315
FAX: 202-225-1101

Rep. Andrew Jacobs, Jr. (D)
(Tenth District)
2313 Rayburn House
Office Building
Washington, D. C. 20515
Phone: 202-225-4011
FAX: 202-226-4093

IOWA
Senators
Senator Charles E. Grassley (R)
135 Hart Senate Office Building
Washington, D. C. 20510
Phone: 202-224-3744
FAX: 202-224-6020

Senator Thomas R. Harkin (D)
531 Hart Senate Office Building
Washington, D. C. 20510
Phone: 202-224-3254
FAX: 202-224-9369

Representatives
Rep. James A. S. Leach (R)
(First District)
2186 Longworth House
Office Building
Washington, D. C. 20515
Phone: 202-225-6576
FAX: 202-226-1278

Rep. Jim Nussle (R)
(Second District)
308 Cannon House
Office Building
Washington, D. C. 20515
Phone: 202-225-2911
FAX: 202-225-9129

Rep. James R. Lightfoot (R)
(Third District)
2444 Rayburn House
Office Building
Washington, D. C. 20515
Phone: 202-225-3806
FAX: 202-225-6973

Rep. Greg Ganske (R)
 (Fourth District)
2373 Rayburn House
Office Building
Washington, D. C. 20515
Phone: 202-225-4426
FAX: (Unlisted)

Rep. Tom Latham (R)
(Fifth District)
418 Cannon House
Office Building
Washington, D. C. 20515
Phone: 202-225-5476
FAX: 202-225-5796

KANSAS
Senators
Senator Robert Dole (R)
141 Hart Senate Office Building
Washington, D. C. 20510
Phone: 202-224-6521
FAX: 202-224-8952

Senator Nancy Landon Kassebaum (R)
302 Russell Senate
Office Building
Washington, D. C. 20510
Phone: 202-224-4774
FAX: 202-224-3514

Representatives
Rep. Charles P. Roberts (R)
(First District)
1125 Longworth House
Office Building
Washington, D. C. 20515
Phone: 202-225-2715
FAX: 202-225-5375

Rep. Sam Brownback (R)
(Second District)
2243 Longworth House
Office Building
Washington, D. C. 20515
Phone: 202-225-6601
FAX: 202-225-1445

Rep. Jan Meyers (R)
(Third District)
2338 Rayburn House
Office Building
Washington, D. C. 20515
Phone: 202-225-2865
FAX: 202-225-0554

Rep. Todd Tiahrt (R)
(Fourth District)
2371 Rayburn House
Office Building
Washington, D. C. 20515
Phone: 202-225-6216
FAX: 202-225-5398

KENTUCKY
Senators
Senator Wendell Hampton Ford
(D) 173A Russell Senate
Office Building
Washington, D. C. 20510
Phone: 202-224-4343
FAX: 202-224-1144

Senator Mitch McConnell (R)
120 Russell Senate Office Building
Washington, D. C. 20510
Phone: 202-224-2541
FAX: 202-224-2499

Rep. Edward Whitfield (R)
(First District)
1533 Longworth House
Office Building
Washington, D. C. 20515
Phone: 202-225-3115
FAX: 202-225-2169

Rep. Ron Lewis (R)
(Second District)
2333 Rayburn House
Office Building
Washington, D. C. 20515
Phone: 202-225-3501
FAX: (Unlisted)

Rep. Mike Ward (D)
(Third District)
2246 Rayburn House
Office Building
Washington, D. C. 20515
Phone: 202-225-5401
FAX:

Rep. Jim Bunning (R)
(Fourth District)
2437 Rayburn House
Office Building
Washington, D. C. 20515
Phone: 202-225-3465
FAX: 202-225-0003

Rep. Harold D. Rogers (R)
(Fifth District)
2468 Cannon House
Office Building
Washington, D. C. 20515
Phone: 202-225-4601
FAX: 202-225-0940

Rep. Scotty Baesler (D)
(Sixth District)
508 Cannon House
Office Building
Washington, D. C. 20515
Phone: 202-225-4706
FAX: 202-225-2122

LOUISIANA
Senators
Senator J. Bennett Johnston, Jr. (D)
136 Hart Senate
Office Building
Washington, D. C. 20510
Phone: 202-224-5824
FAX: 202-224-2952

Senator John B. Breaux (D)
516 Hart Senate Office Building
Washington, D. C. 20510
Phone: 202-224-4623
FAX: 202-224-2435

Representatives
Rep. Robert Livingston, Jr. (R)
(First District)
2368 Longworth House
Office Building
Washington, D. C. 20515
Phone: 202-225-3015
FAX: 202-225-0739

Rep. William J. Jefferson (D)
(Second District)
428 Cannon House
Office Building
Washington, D. C. 20515
Phone: 202-225-6636
FAX: 202-225-1988

Rep. W. J. "Billy" Tauzin (D)
(Third District)
2330 Rayburn House
Office Building
Washington, D. C. 20515
Phone: 202-225-4031
FAX: 202-225-0563

Rep. Cleo Fields (D)
(Fourth District)
513 Cannon House
Office Building
Washington, D. C. 20515
Phone: 202-225-8490
FAX: 220-225-8959

Rep. James O. McCrery, III (R)
(Fifth District)
225 Cannon House Office Building
Washington, D. C. 20515
Phone: 202-225-2777
FAX: 202-225-8039

Rep. Richard H. Baker (R)
(Sixth District)
434 Cannon House
Office Building
Washington, D. C. 20515
Phone: 202-225-3901
FAX: 202-225-7313

Rep. James A. Hayes (D)
(Seventh District)
2432 Rayburn House
Office Building
Washington, D. C. 20515
Phone: 202-225-2031
FAX: 202-225-1175

MAINE
Senators
Senator William S. Cohen (R)
322 Hart Senate Office Building
Washington, D. C. 20510
Phone: 202-224-2523
FAX: 202-224-2693

Senator Olympia Snow (R)
176 Russell Senate
Office Building
Washington, D. C. 20510
Phone: 202-224-5344
FAX: 202-224-6853

Representatives
Rep. James Longley (R)
(First District)
1530 Longworth House
Office Building
Washington, D. C. 20515
Phone: 202-225-6116
FAX: 202-225-9065

Rep. John Baldacci (D)
(Second District)
2268 Rayburn House
Office Building
Washington, D. C. 20515
Phone: 202-225-6306
FAX: 202-225-8297

MARYLAND
Senators
Senator Paul S. Sarbanes (D)
309 Hart Senate Office Building
Washington, D. C. 20510
Phone: 202-224-4524
FAX: 202-224-1651

Senator Barbara A. Mikulski (D)
709 Hart Senate Office Building
Washington, D. C. 20510
Phone: 202-224-4654
FAX: 202-224-8858

Representatives
Rep. Wayne T. Gilchrest (R)
(First District)
412 Cannon House Office Building
Washington, D. C. 20515
Phone: 202-225-5311
FAX: 202-225-0254

Rep. Robert Erlich (R)
(Second District)
1610 Longworth House
Office Building
Washington, D. C. 20515
Phone: 202-225-3061
FAX: 202-225-4251

Rep. Benjamin L. Cardin (D)
(Third District)
227 Cannon House
Office Building
Washington, D. C. 20515
Phone: 202-225-4016
FAX: 202-225-9219

Rep. Albert R. Wynn (D)
(Fourth District)
423 Cannon House
Office Building
Washington, D. C. 20515
Phone: 202-225-8699
FAX: 202-225-8714

Rep. Steny H. Hoyer (D)
(Fifth District)
1705 Longworth House
Office Building
Washington, D. C. 20515
Phone: 202-225-4131
FAX: 202-225-4300

Rep. Roscoe Bartlett (R)
(Sixth District)
312 Cannon House Office
Building
Washington, D. C. 20515
Phone: 202-225-2721
FAX: 202-225-2193

Rep. Kweisi Mfume (D)
(Seventh District)
2419 Rayburn House
Office Building
Washington, D. C. 20515
Phone: 202-225-4741
FAX: 202-225-3178

Rep. Constance A. Morella (R)
(Eighth District)
223 Cannon House
Office Building
Washington, D. C. 20515
Phone: 202-225-5341
FAX: 202-225-1389

MASSACHUSETTS
Senators
Senator Edward M. Kennedy (D)
315 Russell Senate
Office Building
Washington, D. C. 20510
Phone: 202-224-4543
FAX: 202-224-2417

Senator John Kerry (D)
421 Russell Senate
Office Building
Washington, D. C. 20510
Phone: 202-224-2742
FAX: 202-224-8525

Representatives
Rep. John W. Olver (D)
(First District)
1323 Longworth House
Office Building
Washington, D. C. 20515
Phone: 202-225-5335
FAX: 202-226-1224

Rep. Richard E. Neal (D)
(Second District)
131 Cannon House
Office Building
Washington, D. C. 20515
Phone: 202-225-5601
FAX: 202-225-8112

Rep. Peter I. Blute (R)
(Third District)
1029 Longworth House
Office Building
Washington, D. C. 20515
Phone: 202-225-6101
FAX: 202-225-2217

Rep. Barney Frank (D)
(Fourth District)
2404 Rayburn House
Office Building
Washington, D. C. 20515
Phone: 202-225-5931
FAX: 202-225-0182

Rep. Martin T. Meehan (D)
(Fifth District)
1223 Longworth House
Office Building
Washington, D. C. 20515
Phone: 202-225-3411
FAX: 202-225-0771

Rep. Peter G. Torkildsen (R)
(Sixth District)
120 Cannon House
Office Building
Washington, D. C. 20515
Phone: 202-225-8020
FAX: 202-225-8037

Rep. Edward J. Markey (D)
(Seventh District)
2133 Rayburn House
Office Building
Washington, D. C. 20515
Phone: 202-225-2836
FAX: 202-225-8689

Rep. Joseph P. Kennedy, II (D)
(Eighth District)
1210 Longworth House
Office Building
Washington, D. C. 20515
Phone: 202-225-5111
FAX: 202-225-9322

Rep. John J. Moakley (D)
(Ninth District)
235 Cannon House
Office Building
Washington, D. C. 20515
Phone: 202-225-8273
FAX: 202-225-3984

Rep. Gerry E. Studds (D)
(Tenth District)
237 Cannon House
Office Building
Washington, D. C. 20515
Phone: 202-225-3111
FAX: 202-225-2212

MICHIGAN

Senators

Senator Spencer Abraham (R)
105 Dirksen Senate
Office Building
Washington, D. C. 20510
Phone: 202-224-4822
FAX: 202-224-8834

Senator Carl M. Levin (D)
459 Russell Senate
Office Building
Washington, D. C. 20510
Phone: 202-224-6221
FAX: 202-224-5908

Representatives

Rep. Bart Stupak (D)
(First District)
317 Cannon House
Office Building
Washington, D. C. 20515
Phone: 202-225-4735
FAX: 202-225-4744

Rep. Peter Hoekstra (R)
(Second District)
1319 Longworth House
Office Building
Washington, D. C. 20515
Phone: 202-225-4401
FAX: 202-226-0779

Rep. Vernon Ehlers (R)
(Third District)
1526 Longworth House
Office Building
Washington, D. C. 20515
Phone: 202-225-3831
FAX: (Unlisted)

Rep. David Camp (R)
(Fourth District)
137 Cannon House
Office Building
Washington, D. C. 20515
Phone: 202-225-3561
FAX: 202-225-9679

Rep. James A. Barcia (D)
(Fifth District)
1717 Longworth House
Office Building
Washington, D. C. 20515
Phone: 202-225-8171
FAX: 202-225-2168

Rep. Frederick S. Upton (R)
(Sixth District)
2439 Longworth House
Office Building
Washington, D. C. 20515
Phone: 202-225-3761
FAX: 202-225-4986

Rep. Nick Smith (R)
(Seventh District)
1708 Longworth House
Office Building
Washington, D. C. 20515
Phone: 202-225-6276
FAX: 202-225-6281

Rep. Dick Chrysler (R)
(Eighth District)
2347 Rayburn House
Office Building
Washington, D. C. 20515
Phone: 202-225-4872
FAX: 202-225-1260

Rep. Dale E. Kildee (D)
(Ninth District)
2239 Rayburn House
Office Building
Washington, D. C. 20515
Phone: 202-225-3611
FAX: 202-225-6393

Rep. David E. Bonior (D)
(Tenth District)
2207 Rayburn House
Office Building
Washington, D. C. 20515
Phone: 202-225-2106
FAX: 202-226-1169

Rep. Joe Knollenberg (R)
(Eleventh District)
1218 Longworth House
Office Building
Washington, D. C. 20515
Phone: 202-225-5802
FAX: 202-226-2356

Rep. Sander Martin Levin (D)
(Twelfth District)
106 Cannon House
Office Building
Washington, D. C. 20515
Phone: 202-225-4961
FAX: 202-226-1033

Rep. Lynn Rivers (D)
(Thirteenth District)
2107 Rayburn House
Office Building
Washington, D. C. 20515
Phone: 202-225-6261
FAX: 202-225-0489

Rep. John Conyers, Jr. (D)
(Fourteenth District) Rayburn
House
Office Building
Washington, D. C. 20515
Phone: 202-225-5126
FAX: 202-225-0072

Rep. Barbara-Rose Collins (D)
(Fifteenth District)
1108 Longworth House
Office Building
Washington, D. C. 20515
Phone: 202-225-2261
FAX: 202-225-6645

Rep. John D. Dingell (D)
(Sixteenth District)
2328 Rayburn House
Office Building
Washington, D. C. 20515
Phone: 202-225-4071
FAX: 202-225-7426

MINNESOTA

Senators

Senator Rod Grams (R)
154 Russell Senate
Office Building
Washington, D. C. 20510
Phone: 202-224-3244
FAX: 202-224-9931

Senator Paul Wellstone (DFL)
717 Hart Senate
Office Building
Washington, D. C. 20510
Phone: 202-224-5641
FAX: 202-224-8438

Representatives

Rep. Gil Gutknecht (DFL) (First
District)
436 Cannon House
Office Building
Washington, D. C. 20515
Phone: 202-225-2472
FAX: 202-225-0051

Rep. David Minge (D)
(Second District)
1508 Longworth House
Office Building
Washington, D. C. 20515
Phone: 202-225-2331
FAX: 202-226-0836

Rep. James Ramstad (R)
(Third District)
322 Cannon House
Office Building
Washington, D. C. 20515
Phone: 202-225-2871
FAX: 202-225-6351

Rep. Bruce F. Vento (DFL)
(Fourth District)
2304 Rayburn House
Office Building
Washington, D. C. 20515
Phone: 202-225-6631
FAX: 202-225-1968

Rep. Martin Olav Sabo (DFL)
(Fifth District)
2336 Rayburn House
Office Building
Washington, D. C. 20515
Phone: 202-225-4755
FAX: 202-225-4886

Rep. William Luther (D)
(Sixth District)
1713 Longworth House
Office Building
Washington, D. C. 20515
Phone: 202-225-2271
FAX: 202-225-9802

Rep. Collin C. Peterson (DFL)
(Seventh District)
1133 Longworth House
Office Building
Washington, D. C. 20515
Phone: 202-225-2165
FAX: 202-225-1593

Rep. James L. Oberstar (DFL)
(Eighth District)
2366 Rayburn House
Office Building
Washington, D. C. 20515
Phone: 202-225-6211
FAX: 202-225-0699

MISSISSIPPI

Senators
Senator Thad Cochran (R)
326 Russell Senate
Office Building
Washington, D. C. 20510
Phone: 202-224-5054
FAX: 202-224-3576

Senator Trent Lott (R)
487 Russell Senate
Office Building
Washington, D. C. 20510
Phone: 202-224-6253
FAX: 202-224-2262

Representatives
Rep. Roger Wicker (R)
(First District)
2314 Rayburn House
Office Building
Washington, D. C. 20515
Phone: 202-225-4306
FAX: 202-225-4328

Rep. Bennie Thompson (D)
(Second District)
1408 Longworth House
Office Building
Washington, D. C. 20515
Phone: 202-225-5876
FAX: 202-225-5898

Rep. G. V. "Sonny" Montgomery (D) (Third District)
2184 Rayburn House
Office Building
Washington, D. C. 20515
Phone: 202-225-5031
FAX: 202-225-3375

Rep. Mike Parker (D)
(Fourth District)
1410 Longworth House
Office Building
Washington, D. C. 20515
Phone: 202-225-5865
FAX: 202-225-5886

MISSOURI

Senators
Senator John Ashcroft (R)
249 Russell Senate
Office Building
Washington, D. C. 20510
Phone: 202-224-6154
FAX: 202-224-7615

Senator Christopher Samuel "Kit" Bond (R)
293 Russell Senate
Office Building
Washington, D. C. 20510
Phone: 202-224-5721
FAX: 202-224-7491

Representatives
Rep. William L. Clay (D)
(First District)
2306 Rayburn House
Office Building
Washington, D. C. 20515
Phone: 202-225-2406
FAX: 202-225-1725

Rep. James M. Talent (R)
(Second District)
1022 Longworth House
Office Building
Washington, D. C. 20515
Phone: 202-225-2561
FAX: 202-225-2563

Rep. Richard A. Gephardt (D)
(Third District)
1432 Longworth House
Office Building
Washington, D. C. 20515
Phone: 202-225-2671
FAX: 202-225-7414

Rep. Isaac "Ike" Skelton, IV (D)
(Fourth District)
2227 Rayburn House
Office Building
Washington, D. C. 20515
Phone: 202-225-2876
FAX: 202-225-2695

Rep. Karen McCarthy (D)
(Fifth District)
2334 Rayburn House
Office Building
Washington, D. C. 20515
Phone: 202-225-4535
FAX: 202-225-5990

Rep. Pat Danner (D)
(Sixth District)
1217 Longworth House
Office Building
Washington, D. C. 20515
Phone: 202-225-7041
FAX: 202-225-8221

Rep. Melton D. Hancock (R)
(Seventh District)
129 Cannon House
Office Building
Washington, D. C. 20515
Phone: 202-225-6536
FAX: 202-225-7700

Rep. Bill Emerson (R)
(Eighth District)
2454 Cannon House
Office Building
Washington, D. C. 20515
Phone: 202-225-4404
FAX: 202-225-9621

Rep. Harold L. Volkmer (D)
(Ninth District)
2409 Rayburn House
Office Building
Washington, D. C. 20515
Phone: 202-225-2956
FAX: 202-225-7834

MONTANA

Senators
Senator Max Baucus (D)
511 Hart Senate
Office Building
Washington, D. C. 20510
Phone: 202-224-2651
FAX: (Unavailable at T.O.P.)

Senator Conrad Burns (R)
183 Dirksen Senate
Office Building
Washington, D. C. 20510
Phone: 202-224-2644
FAX: 202-224-8594

Representative At Large
Rep. Pat Williams (D)
2457 Rayburn House
Office Building
Washington, D. C. 20515
Phone: 202-225-3211
FAX: 202-226-0244

NEBRASKA

Senators
Senator J. James Exon (D)
528 Hart Senate
Office Building
Washington, D. C. 20510
Phone: 202-224-4224
FAX: 202-224-5213

Senator Joseph R. Kerrey (D)
303 Hart Senate
Office Building
Washington, D. C. 20510
Phone: 202-224-6551
FAX: 202-224-7645

Representatives
Rep. Douglas K. Bereuter (R)
(First District)
2348 Rayburn House
Office Building
Washington, D. C. 20515
Phone: 202-225-4806
FAX: 202-226-1148

Rep. Jon Christensen (R)
(Second District)
1113 Longworth House
Office Building
Washington, D. C. 20515
Phone: 202-225-4155
FAX: 202-225-4684

Rep. William Barrett (R)
(Third District)
1213 Longworth House
Office Building
Washington, D. C. 20515
Phone: 202-225-6435
FAX: 202-225-0207

NEVADA

Senators
Senator Harry M. Reid (D)
324 Hart Senate
Office Building
Washington, D. C. 20510
Phone: 202-224-3542
FAX: 202-224-7327

Senator Richard H. Bryan (D)
364 Russell Senate
Office Building
Washington, D. C. 20510
Phone: 202-224-6244
FAX: 202-224-1867

Representatives
Rep. John Ensign (D)
(First District)
2431 Rayburn House
Office Building
Washington, D. C. 20515
Phone: 202-255-5965
FAX: 202-225-8808

Rep. Barbara F. Vucanovich (R)
(Second District)
2202 Rayburn House Office
Building
Washington, D. C. 20515
Phone: 202-225-6155
FAX: 202-225-2319

NEW HAMPSHIRE
Senators
Senator Judd Gregg (R)
393 Russell Senate
Office Building
Washington, D. C. 20510
Phone: 202-224-3324
FAX: 202-224-4952

Senator Robert C. Smith (R)
332 Dirksen Senate
Office Building
Washington, D. C. 20510
Phone: 202-224-2841
FAX: 202-224-1353

Representatives
Rep. William Zeliff (R)
(First District)
224 Cannon House
Office Building
Washington, D. C. 20515
Phone: 202-225-5456
FAX: 202-225-4370

Rep. Charles Bass (R)
(Second District)
230 Cannon House
Office Building
Washington, D. C. 20515
Phone: 202-225-5206
FAX: 202-225-0046

NEW JERSEY
Senators
Senator Bill Bradley (D)
731 Hart Senate
Office Building
Washington, D. C. 20510
Phone: 202-224-3224
FAX: 202-224-8567

Senator Frank R. Lautenberg
(D) 506 Hart Senate
Office Building
Washington, D. C. 20510
Phone: 202-224-4744
FAX: 202-224-9707

Representatives
Rep. Robert E. Andrews (D)
(First District)
1005 Longworth House
Office Building
Washington, D. C. 20515
Phone: 202-225-6501
FAX: 202-225-6583

Rep. Frank LoBiondo (R)
(Second District)
241 Cannon House
Office Building
Washington, D. C. 20515
Phone: 202-225-6572
FAX: 202-225-8530

Rep. H. James Saxton (R)
(Third District)
438 Cannon House
Office Building
Washington, D. C. 20515
Phone: 202-225-4765
FAX: 202-225-0778

Rep. Christopher H. Smith (R)
(Fourth District)
2353 Rayburn House
Office Building
Washington, D. C. 20515
Phone: 202-225-3765
FAX: 202-225-7768

Rep. Marge S. Roukema (R)
(Fifth District)
2244 Rayburn House
Office Building
Washington, D. C. 20515
Phone: 202-225-4465
FAX: 202-225-9048

Rep. Frank J. Pallone, Jr. (D)
(Sixth District)
420 Cannon House
Office Building
Washington, D. C. 20515
Phone: 202-225-4671
FAX: 202-225-9665

Rep. Bob Franks (R)
(Seventh District)
429 Cannon House
Office Building
Washington, D. C. 20515
Phone: 202-225-5361
FAX: 202-225-9460

Rep. Bill Martini (R)
(Eighth District)
1728 Longworth House
Office Building
Washington, D. C. 20515
Phone: 202-225-5751
FAX: 202-226-2273

Rep. Robert G. Torricelli (D)
(Ninth District)
2159 Rayburn House
Office Building
Washington, D. C. 20515
Phone: 202-225-5061
FAX: 202-225-0843

Rep. Donald M. Payne (D)
(Tenth District)
417 Cannon House
Office Building
Washington, D. C. 20515
Phone: 202-225-3436
FAX: 202-225-4160

Rep. Rodney Frelinghuysen (R)
(Eleventh District)
2447 Rayburn House
Office Building
Washington, D. C. 20515
Phone: 202-225-5034
FAX: 202-225-0658

Rep. Richard Zimmer (R)
(Twelfth District)
228 Cannon House
Office Building
Washington, D. C. 20515
Phone: 202-225-5801
FAX: 202-226-0792

Rep. Robert Menendez (D)
(Thirteenth District)
1531 Longworth House
Office Building
Washington, D. C. 20515
Phone: 202-225-7919
FAX: 202-22-0792

NEW MEXICO
Senators
Senator Pete V. Domenici (R)
427 Dirksen Senate
Office Building
Washington, D. C. 20510
Phone: 202-224-6621
FAX: 202-224-7371

Senator Jeff Bingaman (D)
524 Hart Senate Office Building
Washington, D. C. 20510
Phone: 202-224-5521
FAX: 202-224-1810

Representatives
Rep. Steven H. Schiff (R)
(First District)
1009 Longworth House
Office Building
Washington, D. C. 20515
Phone: 202-225-6316
FAX: 202-225-4975

Rep. Joseph R. Skeen (R)
(Second District)
2367 Rayburn House
Office Building
Washington, D. C. 20515
Phone: 202-225-2365
FAX: 202-225-9599

Rep. Bill Richardson (D)
(Third District)
2349 Rayburn House
Office Building
Washington, D. C. 20515
Phone: 202-225-6190
FAX: 202-225-1950

NEW YORK
Senators
Senator Daniel Patrick
Moynihan (D)
464 Russell Senate
Office Building
Washington, D. C. 20510
Phone: 202-224-4451
FAX: 202-224-9293

Senator Alfonse M. D'Amato (R)
520 Hart Senate
Office Building
Washington, D. C. 20510
Phone: 202-224-6542
FAX: 202-224-5871

Representatives

Rep. Michael Forbes (R)
(First District)
229 Cannon House
Office Building
Washington, D. C. 20515
Phone: 202-225-3826
FAX: 202-225-0776

Rep. Rick Lazio (R)
(Second District)
314 Cannon House
Office Building
Washington, D. C. 20515
Phone: 202-225-3335
FAX: 202-225-4669

Rep. Peter King (R)
(Third District)
118 Cannon House
Office Building
Washington, D. C. 20515
Phone: 202-225-7896
FAX: 202-226-2279

Rep. Daniel Frisa (R)
(Fourth District)
116 Cannon House
Office Building
Washington, D. C. 20515
Phone: 202-225-5516
FAX: 202-225-4672

Rep. Gary L. Ackerman (D)
(Fifth District)
2445 Rayburn House
Office Building
Washington, D. C. 20515
Phone: 202-225-2601
FAX: 202-225-1589

Rep. Floyd H. Flake (D)
(Sixth District)
1035 Longworth House
Office Building
Washington, D. C. 20515
Phone: 202-225-3461
FAX: 202-225-4169

Rep. Thomas J. Manton (D)
(Seventh District)
203 Cannon House
Office Building
Washington, D. C. 20515
Phone: 202-225-3965
FAX: 202-225-1909

Rep. Jerrold Nadler (D)
(Eighth District)
424 Cannon House
Office Building
Washington, D. C. 20515
Phone: 202-225-5635
FAX: 202-225-6923

Rep. Charles E. Schumer (D)
(Ninth District)
2412 Longworth House
Office Building
Washington, D. C. 20515
Phone: 202-225-6616
FAX: 202-225-4183

Rep. Edolphus Towns (D)
(Tenth District)
2232 Rayburn House
Office Building
Washington, D. C. 20515
Phone: 202-225-5936
FAX: 202-225-1018

Rep. Major R. Owens (D)
(Eleventh District)
2305 Rayburn House
Office Building.
Washington, D. C. 20515
Phone: 202-225-6231
FAX: 202-226-0112

Rep. Nydia Velazquez (D)
(Twelfth District)
132 Cannon House
Office Building
Washington, D. C. 20515
Phone: 202-225-2361
FAX: 202-226-0327

Rep. Susan Molinari (R)
(Thirteenth District)
123 Cannon House
Office Building
Washington, D. C. 20515
Phone: 202-225-3371
FAX: 202-226-1272

Rep. Carolyn Maloney (D)
(Fourteenth District)
1504 Longworth House
Office Building
Washington, D. C. 20515
Phone: 202-225-7944
FAX: 202-225-4709

Rep. Charles Bernard Rangel
(D) (Fifteenth District)
2252 Rayburn House
Office Building
Washington, D. C. 20515
Phone: 202-225-4365
FAX: 202-225-0816

Rep. Jose E. Serrano (D)
(Sixteenth District)
336 Cannon House
Office Building
Washington, D. C. 20515
Phone: 202-225-4361
FAX: 202-225-6001

Rep. Eliot L. Engel (D)
(Seventeenth District)
1434 Longworth House
Office Building
Washington, D. C. 20515
Phone: 202-225-2464
FAX: 202-225-5513

Rep. Nita M. Lowey (D)
(Eighteenth District)
1424 Longworth House
Office Building
Washington, D. C. 20515
Phone: 202-225-6506
FAX: 202-225-0546

Rep. Sue Kelly (R)
(Nineteenth District)
2354 Rayburn House
Office Building
Washington, D. C. 20515
Phone: 202-225-5441
FAX: 202-225-0962

Rep. Benjamin A. Gilman (R)
(Twentieth District)
2185 Rayburn House
Office Building
Washington, D. C. 20515
Phone: 202-225-3776
FAX: 202-225-2541

Rep. Michael R. McNulty (D)
(Twenty-First District)
217 Cannon House
Office Building
Washington, D. C. 20515
Phone: 202-225-5076
FAX: 202-225-5077

Rep. Gerald B. H. Solomon (R)
(Twenty-Second District)
2265 Rayburn House
Office Building
Washington, D. C. 20515
Phone: 202-225-5614
FAX: 202-225-5234

Rep. Sherwood L. Boehlert (R)
(Twenty-Third District)
1127 Longworth House
Office Building
Washington, D. C. 20515
Phone: 202-225-3665
FAX: 202-225-1891

Rep. John McHugh (R)
(Twenty-Fourth District)
416 Cannon House
Office Building
Washington, D. C. 20515
Phone: 202-225-4611
FAX: 202-226-0621

Rep. James T. Walsh (R)
(Twenty-Fifth District)
1330 Longworth House
Office Building
Washington, D. C. 20515
Phone: 202-225-3701
FAX: 202-225-4042

Rep. Maurice Hinchey (D)
(Twenty-Sixth District)
1313 Longworth House
Office Building
Washington, D. C. 20515
Phone: 202-225-6335
FAX: 202-226-0774

Rep. L. William Paxon (R)
(Twenty-Seventh District)
1314 Longworth House
Office Building
Washington, D. C. 20515
Phone: 202-225-5265
FAX: 202-225-5910

Rep. Louise M. Slaughter (D)
(Twenty-Eighth District)
2421 Rayburn House Office
Building
Washington, D. C. 20515
Phone: 202-225-3615
FAX: 202-225-7822

Rep. John J. LaFalce (D)
(Twenty-Ninth District)
2310 Rayburn House
Office Building
Washington, D. C. 20515
Phone: 202-225-3231
FAX: 202-225-8693

Rep. Jack Quinn (R)
(Thirtieth District)
331 Cannon House
Office Building
Washington, D. C. 20515
Phone: 202-225-3306
FAX: 202-226-0347

Rep. Amory "Amo" Houghton, Jr. (R) (Thirty-First District)
1110 Longworth House
Office Building
Washington, D. C. 20515
Phone: 202-225-3161
FAX: 202-225-5574

NORTH CAROLINA
Senators
Senator Jesse A. Helms (R)
403 Dirksen Senate
Office Building
Washington, D. C. 20510
Phone: 202-224-6342
FAX: 202-224-7588

Senator Lauch Faircloth (R)
702 Hart Senate
Office Building
Washington, D. C. 20510
Phone: 202-224-3154
FAX: 202-224-7406

Representatives
Rep. Eva Clayton (D)
(First District)
222 Cannon House
Office Building
Washington, D. C. 20515
Phone: 202-225-3101
FAX: 202-225-3354

Rep. Walter Jones (D)
(Second District)
2229 Rayburn House
Office Building
Washington, D. C. 20515
Phone: 202-225-4531
FAX: 202-225-1539

Rep. Walter Jones (R)
(Third District)
2436 Rayburn House
Office Building
Washington, D. C. 20515
Phone: 202-225-3415
FAX: 202-225-0666

Rep. Fred Heineman (D)
(Fourth District)
2458 Rayburn House
Office Building
Washington, D. C. 20515
Phone: 202-225-1784
FAX: 202-225-6314

Rep. Richard Burr (D)
(Fifth District)
2469 Rayburn House
Office Building
Washington, D. C. 20515
Phone: 202-225-2071
FAX: 202-225-4060

Rep. John Howard Coble (R)
(Sixth District)
403 Cannon House
Office Building
Washington, D. C. 20515
Phone: 202-225-3065
FAX: 202-225-8611

Rep. Charles G. Rose, III (D)
(Seventh District)
2230 Rayburn House
Office Building
Washington, D. C. 20515
Phone: 202-225-2731
FAX: 202-225-2470

Rep. W. G. "Bill" Hefner(D) (Eighth District)
2470 Rayburn House
Office Building
Washington, D. C. 20515
Phone: 202-225-3715
FAX: 202-225-4036

Rep. Sue Myrick (R)
(Ninth District)
401 Cannon House
Office Building
Washington, D. C. 20515
Phone: 202-225-1976
FAX: 202-225-8995

Rep. David Funderburk (R)
(Tenth District)
2238 Rayburn House
Office Building
Washington, D. C. 20515
Phone: 202-225-2576
FAX: 202-225-0316

Rep. Charles H. Taylor (R)
(Eleventh District)
516 Cannon House
Office Building
Washington, D. C. 20515
Phone: 202-225-6401
FAX: 202-225-0519

Rep. Melvin Watt (D)
(Twelfth District)
1232 Longworth House
Office Building
Washington, D. C. 20515
Phone: 202-225-1510
FAX: 202-225-1512

NORTH DAKOTA
Senators
Senator Byron L. Dorgan (D)
713 Hart Senate
Office Building
Washington, D. C. 20510
Phone: 202-224-2551
FAX: 202-224-1193

Senator Kent Conrad (D)
724 Hart Senate
Office Building
Washington, D. C. 20510
Phone: 202-224-2043
FAX: 202-224-7776

Representative At Large
Rep. Earl Pomeroy (D)
318 Cannon House
Office Building
Washington, D. C. 20515
Phone: 202-225-2611
FAX: 202-226-0893

OHIO
Senators
Senator John H. Glenn, Jr. (D)
503 Hart Senate
Office Building
Washington, D. C. 20510
Phone: 202-224-3353
FAX: 202-224-7983

Senator Mike DeWine (R)
140 Russell Senate
Office Building
Washington, D. C. 20510
Phone: 202-224-2315
FAX: 202-224-6519

Representatives
Rep. Steve Chabot (D)
(First District)
503 Cannon House
Office Building
Washington, D. C. 20515
Phone: 202-225-2216
FAX: 202-225-4732

Rep. Rob Portman (R)
(Second District)
238 Cannon House
Office Building
Washington, D. C. 20515
Phone: 202-225-3164
FAX: 202-225-1992

Rep. Tony P. Hall (D)
(Third District)
2264 Rayburn House
Office Building
Washington, D. C. 20515
Phone: 202-225-6465
FAX: 202-225-6766

Rep. Michael G. Oxley (R)
(Fourth District)
2233 Rayburn House
Office Building
Washington, D. C. 20515
Phone: 202-225-2676
FAX: 202-226-1160

Rep. Paul E. Gillmor (R)
(Fifth District)
1203 Longworth House
Office Building
Washington, D. C. 20515
Phone: 202-225-6405
FAX: 202-225-1985

Rep. Frank Cremeans (R)
(Sixth District)
1429 Longworth House
Office Building
Washington, D. C. 20515
Phone: 202-225-5705
FAX: 202-226-0331

Rep. David L. Hobson (R)
(Seventh District)
1507 Longworth House
Office Building
Washington, D. C. 20515
Phone: 202-225-4324
FAX: 202-225-1984

Rep. John A. Boehner (R)
(Eighth District)
1020 Longworth House
Office Building
Washington, D. C. 20515
Phone: 202-225-6205
FAX: 202-225-0704

Rep. Marcy Kaptur (D)
(Ninth District)
2104 Rayburn House
Office Building
Washington, D. C. 20515
Phone: 202-225-4146
FAX: 202-225-7711

Rep. Martin R. Hoke (R)
(Tenth District)
212 Cannon House
Office Building
Washington, D. C. 20515
Phone: 202-225-5871
FAX: 202-226-0994

Rep. Louis Stokes (D)
(Eleventh District)
2365 Rayburn House
Office Building
Washington, D. C. 20515
Phone: 202-225-7032
FAX: 202-225-1339

Rep. John R. Kasich (R)
(Twelfth District)
1131 Longworth House
Office Building
Washington, D. C. 20515
Phone: 202-225-5355
FAX: (Unlisted)

Rep. Sherrod Brown (D)
(Thirteenth District)
1407 Longworth House
Office Building
Washington, D. C. 20515
Phone: 202-225-3401
FAX: 202-225-2266

Rep. Thomas C. Sawyer (D)
(Fourteenth District)
1414 Longworth House
Office Building
Washington, D. C. 20515
Phone: 202-225-5231
FAX: 202-225-5278

Rep. Deborah Pryce (R)
(Fifteenth District)
128 Cannon House
Office Building
Washington, D. C. 20515
Phone: 202-225-2015
FAX: 202-226-0986

Rep. Ralph S. Regula (R)
(Sixteenth District)
2309 Rayburn House
Office Building
Washington, D. C. 20515
Phone: 202-225-3876
FAX: 202-225-3059

Rep. James A. Traficant, Jr. (D)
(Seventeenth District)
2446 Rayburn House
Office Building
Washington, D. C. 20515
Phone: 202-225-5261
FAX: 202-225-3719

Rep. E. Bob Ney (R)
(Eighteenth District)
2183 Rayburn House
Office Building
Washington, D. C. 20515
Phone: 202-225-6265
FAX: 202-225-3087

Rep. Steven LaTourette (D)
(Nineteenth District)
431 Cannon House
Office Building
Washington, D. C. 20515
Phone: 202-225-5731
FAX: 202-225-9114

OKLAHOMA
Senators
Senator James InHofe (R)
453 Russell Senate
Office Building
Washington, D. C. 20510
Phone: 202-224-4721
FAX: (Unlisted)

Senator Donald L.Nickles (R)
133 Hart Senate
Office Building
Washington, D. C. 20510
Phone: 202-224-5754
FAX: 202-224-6008

Representatives
Rep. Steve Largent (R)
(First District)
442 Cannon House
Office Building
Washington, D. C. 20515
Phone: 202-225-2211
FAX: 202-225-9187

Rep. Tom Coburn (R)
(Second District)
2329 Rayburn House
Office Building
Washington, D. C. 20515
Phone: 202-225-2701
FAX: 202-225-2796

Rep. William Brewster (D)
(Third District)
1727 Longworth House
Office Building
Washington, D. C. 20515
Phone: 202-225-4565
FAX: 202-225-9029

Rep. J. C. Watts (R)
(Fourth District)
2344 Rayburn House
Office Building
Washington, D. C. 20515
Phone: 202-225-6165
FAX: 202-225-9746

Rep. Earnest J. Istook (R)
(Fifth District)
1116 Longworth House
Office Building
Washington, D. C. 20515
Phone: 202-225-2132
FAX: 202-226-1463

Rep. Frank Lucas (R)
(Sixth District)
2206 Rayburn House
Office Building
Washington, D. C. 20515
Phone: 202-225-5565
FAX: 202-225-8698

OREGON
Senators
Senator Mark O. Hatfield (R)
711 Hart Senate
Office Building
Washington, D. C. 20510
Phone: 202-224-3753
FAX: 202-224-0276

**Senator Robert William
Packwood (R)**
259 Russell Senate
Office Building
Washington, D. C. 20510
Phone: 202-224-5244
FAX: 202-228-3576

Representatives
Rep. Elizabeth Furse (D)
(First District)
316 Cannon House
Office Building
Washington, D. C. 20515
Phone: 202-225-0855
FAX: 202-225-9497

Rep. Wes Cooley (R)
(Second District)
118 Cannon House
Office Building
Washington, D. C. 20515
Phone: 202-225-6730
FAX: 202-225-3129

Rep. Ron Wyden (D)
(Third District)
1111 Longworth House
Office Building
Washington, D. C. 20515
Phone: 202-225-4811
FAX: 202-225-8941

Rep. Peter A. DeFazio (D)
(Fourth District)
1233 Longworth House
Office Building
Washington, D. C. 20515
Phone: 202-225-6416
FAX: 202-225-0694

Rep. Catherine Webber (D)
(Fifth District)
218 Cannon House
Office Building
Washington, D. C. 20510
Phone: 202-225-5711
FAX: 202-225-9477

PENNSYLVANIA
Senators
Senator Rick Santorum (R)
521 Dirksen Senate
Office Building
Washington, D. C. 20510
Phone: 202-224-6324
FAX: 202-224-4161

Senator Arlen Specter (R)
530 Hart Senate
Office Building
Washington, D. C. 20510
Phone: 202-224-4254
FAX: 202-224-1893

Representatives
Rep. Thomas M. Foglietta (D)
(First District)
341 Cannon House
Office Building
Washington, D. C. 20515
Phone: 202-225-4731
FAX: 202-225-0088

Rep. Chaka Fattah (D)
(Second District)
410 Cannon House
Office Building
Washington, D. C. 20515
Phone: 202-225-4001
FAX: 202-225-7362

Rep. Robert A. Borski (D)
(Third District)
2161 Rayburn House
Office Building
Washington, D. C. 20515
Phone: 202-225-8251
FAX: 202-225-4628

Rep. Ron Klink (D)
(Fourth District)
1130 Longworth House
Office Building
Washington, D. C. 20515
Phone: 202-225-2565
FAX: 202-226-2274

Rep. William F. Clinger, Jr. (R)
(Fifth District)
2160 Rayburn House
Office Building
Washington, D. C. 20515
Phone: 202-225-5121
FAX: 202-225-4681

Rep. Tim Holden (D)
(Sixth District)
1421 Longworth House
Office Building
Washington, D. C. 20515
Phone: 202-225-5546
FAX: 202-226-0996

Rep. Wayne C. Weldon (R)
(Seventh District)
2452 Cannon House
Office Building
Washington, D. C. 20515
Phone: 202-225-2011
FAX: 202-225-8137

Rep. Jim Greenwood (R)
(Eighth District)
515 Cannon House
Office Building
Washington, D. C. 20515
Phone: 202-225-4276
FAX: 202-225-9511

Rep. E. G. "Bud" Shuster (R)
(Ninth District)
2188 Rayburn House
Office Building
Washington, D. C. 20515
Phone: 202-225-2431
FAX: 202-225-2486

Rep. Joseph M. McDade (R)
(Tenth District)
2370 Rayburn House
Office Building
Washington, D. C. 20515
Phone: 202-225-3731
FAX: 202-225-9594

Rep. Paul E. Kanjorski (D)
(Eleventh District)
2429 Cannon House
Office Building
Washington, D. C. 20515
Phone: 202-225-6511
FAX: 202-225-9024

Rep. John P. Murtha (D)
(Twelfth District)
2423 Rayburn House
Office Building
Washington, D. C. 20515
Phone: 202-225-2065
FAX: 202-225-5709

Rep. Jon Fox (R)
(Thirteenth District)
1516 Rayburn House
Office Building
Washington, D. C. 20515
Phone: 202-225-6111
FAX: 202-226-0798

Rep. William J. Coyne (D)
(Fourteenth District)
2455 Rayburn House
Office Building
Washington, D. C. 20515
Phone: 202-225-2301
FAX: 202-225-1844

Rep. Paul McHale (D)
(Fifteenth District)
511 Rayburn House
Office Building
Washington, D. C. 20515
Phone: 202-225-6411
FAX: 202-225-5320

Rep. Robert S. Walker (R)
(Sixteenth District)
2369 Rayburn House
Office Building
Washington, D. C. 20515
Phone: 202-225-2411
FAX: 202-225-2484

Rep. George W. Gekas (R)
(Seventeenth District)
2410 Longworth House
Office Building
Washington, D. C. 20515
Phone: 202-225-4315
FAX: 202-225-8440

Rep. Michael Doyle (D)
(Eighteenth District)
1222 Longworth House
Office Building
Washington, D. C. 20515
Phone: 202-225-2135
FAX: 202-225-7747

Rep. William F. Goodling (R)
(Nineteenth District)
2263 Rayburn House
Office Building
Washington, D. C. 20515
Phone: 202-225-5836
FAX: 202-226-1000

Rep. Frank Mascara (D)
(Twentieth District)
2210 Rayburn House
Office Building
Washington, D. C. 20515
Phone: 202-225-4665
FAX: 202-225-4772

Rep. Philip English (R)
(Twenty-First District)
1714 Longworth House
Office Building
Washington, D. C. 20515
Phone: 202-225-5406
FAX: 202-225-1081

RHODE ISLAND
Senators
Senator Claiborne Pell (D)
335 Russell Senate
Office Building
Washington, D. C. 20510
Phone: 202-224-4642
FAX: 202-224-4680

Senator John H. Chafee (R)
567 Dirksen Senate
Office Building
Washington, D. C. 20510
Phone: 202-224-2921
FAX: 202-224-7472

Representatives
Rep. Patrick Kennedy (D)
(First District)
326 Cannon House
Office Building
Washington, D. C. 20515
Phone: 202-225-4911
FAX: 202-225-4417

Rep. John F. Reed (R)
(Second District)
1510 Longworth House
Office Building
Washington, D. C. 20515
Phone: 202-225-2735
FAX: 202-225-9580

SOUTH CAROLINA

Senators

Senator James Strom Thurmond (R)
217 Russell Senate
Office Building
Washington, D. C. 20510
Phone: 202-224-5972
FAX: 202-224-1300

Senator Ernest F. Hollings (D)
125 Russell Senate
Office Building
Washington, D. C. 20510
Phone: 202-224-6121
FAX: 202-224-3573

Representatives

Rep. Mark Sanford (R)
(First District)
231 Cannon House
Office Building
Washington, D. C. 20515
Phone: 202-225-3176
FAX: 202-225-4340

Rep. Floyd D. Spence (R)
(Second District)
2405 Rayburn House
Office Building
Washington, D. C. 20515
Phone: 202-225-2452
FAX: 202-225-2455

Rep. Lindsey Graham (R)
(Third District)
221 Cannon House
Office Building
Washington, D. C. 20515
Phone: 202-225-5301
FAX: 202-225-5383

Rep. Bob Inglis (R)
(Fourth District)
1237 Longworth House
Office Building
Washington, D. C. 20515
Phone: 202-225-6030
FAX: 202-226-1177

Rep. John M. Spratt, Jr. (D)
(Fifth District)
1536 Longworth House
Office Building
Washington, D. C. 20515
Phone: 202-225-5501
FAX: 202-225-0464

Rep. James E. Clyburn (D)
(Sixth District)
319 Cannon House
Office Building
Washington, D. C. 20515
Phone: 202-225-3315
FAX: 202-225-2313

SOUTH DAKOTA

Senators

Senator Larry Pressler (R)
283 Rayburn House
Office Building
Washington, D. C. 20510
Phone: 202-224-5842
FAX: 202-224-1630

Senator Thomas Andrew Daschle (D)
317 Hart Senate
Office Building
Washington, D. C. 20510
Phone: 202-224-2321
FAX: 202-224-2047

Representative At Large

Rep. Timothy P. Johnson (D)
2438 Rayburn House
Office Building
Washington, D. C. 20515
Phone: 202-225-2801
FAX: 202-225-2427

TENNESSEE

Senators

Senator Fred Thompson (R)
363 Russell Senate
Office Building
Washington, D. C. 20510
Phone: 202-224-3344
FAX: 202-224-8062

Senator Bill Frist (R)
506 Dirksen Senate
Office Building
Washington, D. C. 20510
Phone: 202-224-1036
FAX: 202-228-3679

Representatives

Rep. James H. Quillen (R)
(First District)
102 Cannon House
Office Building
Washington, D. C. 20515
Phone: 202-225-6356
FAX: 202-225-7812

Rep. John J. Duncan, Jr. (R)
(Second District)
115 Cannon House
Office Building
Washington, D. C. 20515
Phone: 202-225-5435
FAX: 202-225-6440

Rep. Zach Wamp (R)
(Third District)
2406 Rayburn House
Office Building
Washington, D. C. 20515
Phone: 202-225-3271
FAX: 202-225-6974

Rep. Van Hilleary (R)
(Fourth District)
125 Cannon House
Office Building
Washington, D. C. 20515
Phone: 202-225-6831
FAX: 202-225-4520

Rep. Bob Clement (D)
(Fifth District)
1230 Cannon House
Office Building
Washington, D. C. 20515
Phone: 202-225-4311
FAX: 202-226-1035

Rep. Barton J. Gordon (D)
(Sixth District)
103 Cannon House
Office Building
Washington, D. C. 20515
Phone: 202-225-4231
FAX: 202-225-6887

Rep. Ed Bryant (R)
(Seventh District)
339 Cannon House
Office Building
Washington, D. C. 20515
Phone: 202-225-2811
FAX: 202-225-2814

Rep. John S. Tanner (D)
(Eighth District)
1427 Longworth House
Office Building
Washington, D. C. 20515
Phone: 202-225-4714
FAX: 202-225-1765

Rep. Harold Eugene Ford (D)
(Ninth District)
2211 Rayburn House
Office Building
Washington, D. C. 20515
Phone: 202-225-3265
FAX: 202-225-9215

TEXAS

Senators

Senator Phil Gramm (R)
370 Russell Senate
Office Building
Washington, D. C. 20510
Phone: 202-224-2934
FAX: 202-228-2856

Senator Kathyrn "Kay" Bailey Hutchison (R)
703 Hart Senate Office Building
Washington, D. C. 20510
Phone: 202-224-5922
FAX: 202-224-0776

Representatives

Rep. Jim Chapman (D)
(First District)
2417 Rayburn House
Office Building
Washington, D. C. 20515
Phone: 202-225-3035
FAX: 202-225-7265

Rep. Charles N. Wilson (D)
(Second District)
2256 Rayburn House
Office Building
Washington, D. C. 20515
Phone: 202-225-2401
FAX: 202-225-1764

Rep. Sam Johnson (R)
(Third District)
1030 Longworth House
Office Building
Washington, D. C. 20515
Phone: 202-225-4201
FAX: 202-225-1485

Rep. Ralph M. Hall (D)
(Fourth District)
2236 Rayburn House
Office Building
Washington, D. C. 20515
Phone: 202-225-6673
FAX: 202-225-3332

Rep. John Wiley Bryant (D)
(Fifth District)
205 Cannon House
Office Building
Washington, D. C. 20515
Phone: 202-225-2231
FAX: 202-225-9721

Rep. Joe Linus Barton (R)
(Sixth District)
1514 Longworth House
Office Building
Washington, D. C. 20515
Phone: 202-225-2002
FAX: 202-225-3052

Rep. Bill Archer (R)
(Seventh District)
1236 Longworth House
Office Building
Washington, D. C. 20515
Phone: 202-225-2571
FAX: 202-225-4381

Rep. Jack Fields (R)
(Eighth District)
2228 Rayburn House
Office Building
Washington, D. C. 20515
Phone: 202-225-4901
FAX: 202-225-2772

Rep. Steve Stockman (R)
(Ninth District)
2449 Rayburn Hous
Office Building
Washington, D. C. 20515
Phone: 202-225-6565
FAX: 202-225-1584

Rep. Lloyd Doggett (D)
(Tenth District)
242 Cannon House
Office Building
Washington, D. C. 20515
Phone: 202-225-4865
FAX: 202-225-3018

Rep. Chet Edwards (D)
(Eleventh District)
328 Cannon House
Office Building
Washington, D. C. 20515
Phone: 202-225-6105
FAX: 202-225-0350

Rep. Preston M. "Pete" Geren
(D) (Twelfth District)
1730 Longworth House
Office Building
Washington, D. C. 20515
Phone: 202-225-5071
FAX: 202-225-2786

Rep. William Thornberry (R)
(Thirteenth District)
126 Cannon House
Office Building
Washington, D. C. 20515
Phone: 202-225-3706
FAX: 202-225-6142

Rep. Greg Laughlin (D)
(Fourteenth District)
236 Cannon House
Office Building
Washington, D. C. 20515
Phone: 202-225-2831
FAX: 202-225-1108

Rep. E. "Kika" de la Garza (D)
(Fifteenth District)
1401 Longworth House
Office Building
Washington, D. C. 20515
Phone: 202-225-2531
FAX: 202-225-2534

Rep. Ronald D'Emory
Coleman (D)
(Sixteenth District)
440 Cannon House
Office Building
Washington, D. C. 20515
Phone: 202-225-4831
FAX: 202-225-4831

Rep. Charles W. Stenholm (D)
(Seventeenth District)
1211 Longworth House
Office Building
Washington, D. C. 20515
Phone: 202-225-6605
FAX: 202-225-2234

Rep. Shelia Lee (D)
(Eighteenth District)
1711 Longworth House
Office Building
Washington, D. C. 20515
Phone: 202-225-3816
FAX: 202-225-6186

Rep. Larry Ed Combest (R)
(Nineteenth District)
1511 Longworth House
Office Building
Washington, D. C. 20515
Phone: 202-225-4005
FAX: 202-225-9615

Rep. Henry B. Gonzalez (D)
(Twentieth District)
2413 Rayburn House
Office Building
Washington, D. C. 20515
Phone: 202-225-3236
FAX: 202-225-1915

Rep. Lamar S. Smith (R)
(Twenty-First District)
2443 Rayburn House
Office Building
Washington, D. C. 20515
Phone: 202-225-4236
FAX: 202-225-8628

Rep. Tom DeLay (R)
(Twenty-Second District)
407 Cannon House
Office Building
Washington, D. C. 20515
Phone: 202-225-5951
FAX: 202-225-5241

Rep. Henry Bonilla (R)
(Twenty-Third District)
1529 Longworth House
Office Building
Washington, D. C. 20515
Phone: 202-225-4511
FAX: 202-225-2237

Rep. Martin Frost (D)
(Twenty-Fourth District)
2459 Rayburn House
Office Building
Washington, D. C. 20515
Phone: 202-225-3605
FAX: 202-225-4951

Rep. Ken Bentsen (D)
(Twenty-Fifth District)
303 Cannon House
Office Building
Washington, D. C. 20515
Phone: 202-225-7508
FAX: 202-225-4210

Rep. Richard K. Armey (R)
(Twenty-Sixth District)
301 Cannon House
Office Building
Washington, D. C. 20515
Phone: 202-225-7772
FAX: 202-225-7614

Rep. Solomon P. Ortiz (D)
(Twenty-Seventh District)
2136 Rayburn House
Office Building
Washington, D. C. 20515
Phone: 202-225-7742
FAX: 202-226-1134

Rep. Frank Tejeda (D)
(Twenty-Eighth District)
323 Cannon House
Office Building
Washington, D. C. 20515
Phone: 202-225-1640
FAX: 202-225-1641

Rep. Gene Green (D)
(Twenty-Ninth District)
1004 Longworth House
Office Building
Washington, D. C. 20515
Phone: 202-225-1688
FAX: 202-225-9903

Rep. Eddie B. Johnson (D)
(Thirtieth District)
1721 Longworth House
Office Building
Washington, D. C. 20515
Phone: 202-225-8885
FAX: 202-226-1477

UTAH

Senators
Senator Robert Bennett (R)
241 Dirksen Senate
Office Building
Washington, D. C. 20510
Phone: 202-224-5444
FAX: 202-224-6717

Senator Orrin G. Hatch (R)
135 Russell Senate
Office Building
Washington, D. C. 20510
Phone: 202-224-5251
FAX: 202-224-6331

Representatives

Rep. James V. Hansen (R)
(First District)
2466 Rayburn House
Office Building
Washington, D. C. 20515
Phone: 202-225-0453
FAX: 202-225-5857

Rep. Karen Shepherd (D)
(Second District)
414 Cannon House
Office Building
Washington, D. C. 20515
Phone: 202-225-3011
FAX: 202-226-0354

Rep. William Orton (D)
(Third District)
1122 Longworth House
Office Building
Washington, D. C. 20515
Phone: 202-225-7751
FAX: 202-226-1223

VERMONT
Senators

Senator Patrick Leahy (D)
433 Russell Senate
Office Building
Washington, D. C. 20510
Phone: 202-224-4242
FAX: 202-224-3595

Senator James M. Jeffords (R)
513 Hart Senate
Office Building
Washington, D. C. 20510
Phone: 202-224-5141
FAX: 202-224-8330

Representative At Large
Rep. Bernard Sanders (Soc)
213 Cannon House
Office Building
Washington, D. C. 20515
Phone: 202-225-4115
FAX: 202-225-6790

VIRGINIA
Senators
Senator John W. Warner (R)
225 Russell Senate
Office Building
Washington, D. C. 20510
Phone: 202-224-2023
FAX: 202-224-6295

Senator Charles S. Robb (D)
493 Russell Senate
Office Building
Washington, D. C. 20510
Phone: 202-224-4024
FAX: 202-224-8689

Representatives

Rep. Herbert H. Bateman (R)
(First District)
2350 Rayburn House
Office Building
Washington, D. C. 20515
Phone: 202-225-4261
FAX: 202-225-4382

Rep. Owen B. Pickett (D)
(Second District)
2430 Rayburn House
Office Building
Washington, D. C. 20515
Phone: 202-225-4215
FAX: 202-225-4218

Rep. Robert C. Scott (D)
(Third District)
501 Cannon House
Office Building
Washington, D. C. 20515
Phone: 202-225-8351
FAX: 202-225-8354

Rep. Norman Sisisky (D)
(Fourth District)
2352 Cannon House
Office Building
Washington, D. C. 20515
Phone: 202-225-6365
FAX: 202-226-1170

Rep. Lewis F. Payne, Jr. (D)
(Fifth District)
1119 Longworth House
Office Building
Washington, D. C. 20515
Phone: 202-225-4711
FAX: 202-226-1147

Rep. Robert W. Goodlatte (R)
(Sixth District)
214 Cannon House
Office Building
Washington, D. C. 20515
Phone: 202-225-5431
FAX: 202-225-9681

Rep. Thomas J. Bliley, Jr. (R)
(Seventh District)
2241 Rayburn House
Office Building
Washington, D. C. 20515
Phone: 202-225-2815
FAX: 202-225-0011

Rep. James P. Moran, Jr. (D)
(Eighth District)
430 Cannon House
Office Building
Washington, D. C. 20515
Phone: 202-225-4376
FAX: 202-225-0017

Rep. Rick Boucher (D)
(Ninth District)
2245 Rayburn House
Office Building
Washington, D. C. 20515
Phone: 202-225-3861
FAX: 202-225-0442

Rep. Frank R. Wolf (R)
(Tenth District)
104 Cannon House
Office Building
Washington, D. C. 20515
Phone: 202-225-5136
FAX: 202-225-0437

Rep. Thomas Davis (R)
(Eleventh District)
1609 Longworth House
Office Building
Washington, D. C. 20515
Phone: 202-225-1492
FAX: 202-225-2274

WASHINGTON
Senators
Senator Patty Murray (D)
302 Hart Senate
Office Building
Washington, D. C. 20510
Phone: 202-224-2621
FAX: 202-224-0238

Senator Slade Gorton (R)
730 Hart Senate
Office Building
Washington, D. C. 20510
Phone: 202-224-3441
FAX: 202-224-9393

Representatives

Rep.Rick White (R)
(First District)
1520 Longworth House
Office Building
Washington, D. C. 20515
Phone: 202-225-6311
FAX: 202-225-2286

Rep. Jack Metcalf (R)
(Second District)
1502 Longworth House
Office Building
Washington, D. C. 20515
Phone: 202-225-2605
FAX: 202-225-2608

Rep. Linda Smith (R)
(Third District)
1527 Longworth House
Office Building
Washington, D. C. 20515
Phone: 202-225-3536
FAX: 202-225-9095

Rep. Doc Hastings (R)
(Fourth District)
1431 Longworth House
Office Building
Washington, D. C. 20515
Phone: 202-225-5816
FAX: 202-226-1137

Rep. George Nethercutt (R)
(Fifth District)
1201 Longworth House
Office Building
Washington, D. C. 20515
Phone: 202-225-2006
FAX: 202-225-7181

Rep. Norman D. Dicks (D)
(Sixth District)
2467 Rayburn House
Office Building
Washington, D. C. 20515
Phone: 202-225-5916
FAX: 202-226-1176

Rep. James A. McDermott
(D) (Seventh District)
1707 Longworth House
Office Building
Washington, D. C. 20515
Phone: 202-225-3106
FAX: 202-225-9212

Rep. Jennifer Dunn (R)
(Eighth District)
1641 Longworth House
Office Building
Washington, D. C. 20515
Phone: 202-225-7761
FAX: 202-225-8673

Rep. Randy Tate (R)
(Ninth District)
1535 Longworth House
Office Building
Washington, D. C. 20515
Phone: 202-225-8901
FAX: 202-226-2361

WEST VIRGINIA
<u>Senators</u>
Senator Robert C. Byrd (D)
311 Hart Senate Office Building
Washington, D. C. 20510
Phone: 202-224-3954
FAX: 202-224-4025

Senator John D. Rockefeller, IV (D)
109 Hart Senate Office Building
Washington, D. C. 20510
Phone: 202-224-6472
FAX: 202-224-7665

<u>Representatives</u>
Rep. Alan B. Mollohan (D)
(First District)
2242 Rayburn House
Office Building
Washington, D. C. 20515
Phone: 202-225-4172
FAX: 202-225-7564

Rep. Robert W. Wise (D)
(Second District)
2434 Rayburn House
Office Building
Washington, D. C. 20515
Phone: 202-225-2711
FAX: 202-225-7856

Rep. Nick Joe Rahall, II (D)
(Third District)
2269 Rayburn House
Office Building
Washington, D. C. 20515
Phone: 202-225-3452
FAX: 202-225-9061

WISCONSIN
<u>Senators</u>
Senator Russell Feingold (D)
502 Hart Senate
Office Building
Washington, D. C. 20510
Phone: 202-224-5323
FAX: 202-224-2725

Senator Herb Kohl (D)
330 Hart Senate
Office Building
Washington, D. C. 20510
Phone: 202-224-5653
FAX: 202-224-9787

<u>Representatives</u>
Rep. Mark Neumann (R)
(First District)
1719 Longworth House
Office Building
Washington, D. C. 20515
Phone: 202-225-3031
FAX: 202-225-9820

Rep. Scott L. Klug (R)
(Second District)
1224 Longworth House
Office Building
Washington, D. C. 20515
Phone: 202-225-2906
FAX: 202-225-6942

Rep. Steven C. Gunderson
(R) (Third District)
2235 Rayburn House
Office Building
Washington, D. C. 20515
Phone: 202-225-5506
FAX: 202-225-6195

Rep. Gerald D. Kleczka (D)
(Fourth District)
2301 Rayburn House
Office Building
Washington, D. C. 20515
Phone: 202-225-4572
FAX: 202-225-0719

Rep. Thomas M. Barrett (D)
(Fifth District)
313 Cannon House
Office Building
Washington, D. C. 20515
Phone: 202-225-3571
FAX: 202-225-2185

Rep. Thomas E. Petri (R)
(Sixth District)
2262 Rayburn House
Office Building
Washington, D. C. 20515
Phone: 202-225-2476
FAX: 202-225-2356

Rep. David R. Obey (D)
(Seventh District)
2462 Rayburn House
Office Building
Washington, D. C. 20515
Phone: 202-225-3365
FAX: 202-225-0561

Rep. Toby Roth (R)
(Eighth District)
2234 Rayburn House
Office Building
Washington, D. C. 20515
Phone: 202-225-5665
FAX: 202-225-0087

Rep. E. James
Sensenbrenner, Jr. (R)
(Ninth District)
2332 Rayburn House
Office Building
Washington, D. C. 20515
Phone: 202-225-5101
FAX: 202-225-3190

WYOMING
<u>Senators</u>
Senator Craig Thomas (R)
237 Russell Senate
Office Building
Washington, D. C. 20510
Phone: 202-224-6441
FAX: 202-224-3230

Senator Alan K. Simpson (R)
261 Dirksen Senate
Office Building
Washington, D. C. 20510
Phone: 202-224-3424
FAX: 202-224-1315

<u>Representative At Large</u>
Rep. Barbara Cubin (R)
1019 Longworth
House Office Building
Washington, D. C. 20505
Phone: 202-225-2311
FAX: 202-225-0726

BIBLIOGRAPHY

Adler, T. and R. Cowen. "Proposed Federal Budget Keeps R&D Afloat." *Science News.* (February 12, 1994) p. 103.

Aburdene, Particia and John Naisbitt. *Megatrends 2000.* William Morrow and Company: New York, 1990.

Austin, Nancy and Tom Peters. *A Passion for Excellence.* Random House: New York, 1985.

Bannock, Graham and R.E. Baxter and Evan Davis. *Dictionary of Economics.* Penguin: London, 1987.

" Best Annual Reports." *Chief Executive Officer.* (October 1992) pp. 26-34.

Bernstein, Aaron. " Inequality," *Business Week.* (August 15, 1994) pp. 78-83

Blaug, Mark. *Great Economist Since Keynes .* Cambridge University Press: Cambridge, 1985.

Calleo, David. *The Bankrupting of America.* Avon Books: New York, 1992.

Caplan, Richard and John Fetter. *State of the Union 1994.* Westiew Press: Boulder, 1994.

Colson, Chuck. *Why America Doesn't Work.* Word Publishing: Dallas. 1991.

"Dollar's Chief Executive Problem." *Forbes* (July 18, 1994) p. 37

Choate, Pat. *Agents of Influence.* Simon and Schuster: New York, 1990.

Dornbusch, Rudiger and F. Leslie Helmers. *The Open Economy.* Oxford University Press: New York: 1988.

Drucker, Peter. *The New Realities.* Harper and Row: New York, 1989.

Feldstein, Martin. *American Economic Policy in the 1980s* National Bureau of Economic Research: Cambridge, 1994.

Economic Report of the President 1994. National Council of Economic Advisors: Transmitted to the Congress of the United States.

Economic Report of the President 1993. National Council of Economic Advisors: Transmitted to the Congress of the United States.

Economic Report of the President 1992. National Council of Economic Advisors: Transmitted to the Congress of the United States.

Friedman, Milton. *Capitalism and Freedom.* University of Chicago Press: Chicago, 1982.

Figgie, Harry E. *Bankruptcy 1995.* Little, Brown and Company: Boston, 1992.

Gaebler, Ted and David Osborne. *Reinventing Government.* Penguin: New York, 1993.

Galbraith, John Kenneth. *The New Industrial State.* Houghton Mifflin: Boston, 1967.

Garreau, Joel. *Edge City.* Doubleday: New York, 1988.

Kanter, Rosabeth M. and Barry A. Stein and Todd D. Jick. *The Challenge of Organizational Change.* Free Press: New York, 1992.

Kidder, Rushworth. *An Agenda for the 21st Century.* MIT Press: Cambridge, 1988.

Kidder, Rushwork. *Reinventing the Future.* MIT Press: Cambridge, 1989.

Kuttner, Robert. "The Big Snag in the Global Economy." *Business Week.* (August 1, 1994) p. 16.

Heilbroner, Robert and Lester Thurow. *Economics Explained.* Simon Schuster: New York, 1994.

Information Alamanac 1994. Houghton Mifflin: Boston, 1994.

"Major Departure in Services," *Forbes.* (July 4, 1994) p. 37.

Marshall, Will and Martin Schram. *Mandate for Change.* Berkeley Books: New York, 1993.

"New Economy: A Special Report." *Fortune.* (June 27, 1994). pp. 36-97.

New Tax Law." *Ernst and Young.* John Wiley and Sons: New York, 1993.

Nixon, Richard. *Beyond Peace.* Random House: New York, 1994.

Nobelists Rate Clintonomics." *Wall Street Journal.* (March 23, 1993) A14:3.

Phillips, Kevin. *Politics of the Rich and Poor.* HarperCollins: New York, 1989.

Piore, Michael and Charles Sabel. *The Second Industrial Divide.* HarperCollins: New York, 1984.

Porter, Michael E. *Competitive Advantage.* Free Press: New York, 1985.

Porter, Michael E. *Competitive Advantage of Nations.* Free Press: New York, 1990.

Porter, Michael E. *Competitive Strategy.* Free Press: New York, 1980.

Portrait of America." *Business Week/ Reinventing America 1992.*

Reich, Robert B. *The Work of Nations.* Alfred A. Knopf, Inc.: New York, 1991.

Saving Our Schools," *Business Week.* (September 14, 1992) pp.70-80.

Schlesinger, Arthur M. *The Disuniting of America.*
W•W Norton and Company: New York, 1992.

Thurow, Lester. *Head to Head.* Time Warner: New York, 1993.

Toffler, Alvin. *Power Shift.* Bantam Books: New York, 1990.

Understanding Our Century. Christian Science Monitor: 1984.

Universal Almanac 1994. Universal Press: Kansas City, 1994.

Vital Statistics. The Economist. Random House: New York, 1990

Weinberger, Casper. "A Domestic Foreign Policy," *Forbes* (July 4, 1994) p.35.

"Why We Feel So Bad." *Forbes.* (February 14, 1993) pp. 47-318.

World Alamanc 1994. Funk and Wagnalls. Mahwah, NJ, 1994.

Bibliography

Special Thanks

*My greatest appreciation to **Mr. Ross Perot** for inspiring America and me to seek accountability from government and for taking my Annual Report before the Congress.*

*The author wishes to offer special thanks to: her father, **Joseph R. Bagby,** for his unending assistance on this report; her mother, **Martha G. Bagby,** for her creative and editing support; her maternal grandmother, **Louise L. Green,** for her encouragement.*

*Many thanks to **Mrs. Kathryn Brookins**, the mother of my roommate, **Laura**, for bringing media attention to my report. And to my lifelong friend and roommate, **Nicole Anzuoni**, for all her support, to **Ms. Doe Coover**, my agent, for believing in my report, to **Ms. Chrissy DeNitto** for her constant help in production and to **Ms. Bonnie Cazin** for her excellent research assistance.*

*Special acknowledgments go to **Dr. Hendrik Houthakker,** Harvard professor of economics, for his mentoring and instruction; **Dr. Dan Feenberg,** the National Bureau of Economic Research, for his guidance in the art of research; **Dr. Martin Feldstein,** Harvard professor of economics, Nobel laureate and president of the National Bureau of Economic Research, for inspiring the author in economics; **Dr. Ben Friedman,** Harvard professor of economics, for his teaching.*

***Mrs. Aileen Josephs,** attorney, Florida Rural Legal Services, Palm Beach County, Fla., for her training and support; **Mr. David Bludworth,** former State's Attorney, Palm Beach County, for his belief in aspiring attorneys; **Mr. Dale Buckner,** attorney, State's Attorney's Office, Palm Beach County, for his court training; **Mr. Gary Adkin,** vice president, JP Morgan Florida, for his guidance in business research; **Mr. Lawrence Miller,** president, Bradley Real Estate Trust, for confidence shown in the author's research and writing.*

***Ms. Fran Carlton,** American Legion Post 12, West Palm Beach, Fla., for demonstrating the highest ideals of American citizenship; **Mr. Ralph Greco, Ms. Glenda Thompson, Mrs. Lynn Dell'Orfano, Mrs. Nora Ugalde, Mrs. Carol Bayless, Mr. Robert Bayless** and in memory of **Mr. Walter H. Butler, Jr.,** former teachers, for imparting the highest educational standards.*

COMING SOON . . .

The Next Annual Report
of the United States of America

Available in in your bookstores in time for the 1996 Presidental Election.

•An in-depth evaluation of the Republicans' Contract with America.

•The announced Presidential candidates' views on the budget, taxes, reducing our deficit, spending and more.

•A complete look at the welfare system in America and how it is being changed.

•World Markets and how they are affecting America.

•Plus more tables, graphs, and summaries to help you better understand where your taxes are spent by the federal government.

•And international and social highlights of the year in review.

Dear Reader:

Your are a SHAREHOLDER in America through the payment of your taxes. It is our job to see that the government we own is managed properly, efficiently, and honestly. I have tried in this report to give you the facts and information, free from political opinion, so you can make your own decision when you exercise your vote about how leaders are performing, particularly in budgeting and spending.

This is meant to be an interactive publication. I need your advice to make this publication better in future additions. We plan to make this an annual report to you. Please give me your suggestions and your advice by writing to:

HarperBusiness
A Division of HarperCollins Publishers
10 East 53rd Street
New York, NY 10022-5299

Attn: Meredith E. Bagby
Annual Report of the U.S.A.